COLLEGE NOT REQUIRED

· ·

Leonard Corwen

MACMILLAN•USA

Copyright ©1995 by Bernice Corwen
All rights reserved
including the right of reproduction
in whole or in part in any form.

Macmillan General Reference
A Simon & Schuster Macmillan Company
1633 Broadway
New York, NY 10019

An Arco Book

MACMILLAN is a registered trademark of Macmillan, Inc.
ARCO is a registered trademark of Prentice-Hall, Inc.

Library of Congress Cataloging-in-Publication Data
Corwen, Leonard.
College not required / Leonard Corwen.
p.   cm.
"An Arco book"—T.p. verso.
ISBN: 0-02-860561-6
1.   Vocational guidance—United States. 2. Occupations—
United States [1. High school graduates—Employment—
United States.]
I. Title.
HF5382.5.U5C669   1995
331.7'02—dc20   95–15933
                                                        CIP

Manufactured in the United States of America

10 9 8 7 6 5 4 3 2

CONTENTS

• •

JOB FINDER
• •

ACKNOWLEDGMENTS

• •

With appreciation . . .

To my wife, Bernice, for her capable assistance in the research and the preparation of the manuscript;

To Carol, for her creative ideas and suggestions;

And to the U.S. Bureau of Labor Statistics who, through their publications and periodicals, provided much of the information, statistics, and sources contained in these pages.

NOTE:
Occupational information contained in this book presents a general, composite description of jobs, and cannot be expected to reflect work situations or salaries and wages paid by specific establishments or localities. Inclusion of a career description or source of information does not constitute a recommendation. The reader must do further research to determine if a job or career is the right choice. The trade associations, professional societies, unions, industrial organizations, and government agencies are listed at the end of each job description as a possible source of information. The author cannot guarantee the accuracy of such information. The listing of an organization does not constitute an endorsement or recommendation either of the organization and its activities or of the information it may supply. Further, the book is not intended and should not be used as a guide for determining wages, hours, or the right of a particular union to represent workers, or formal job evaluation systems. Nor should earnings data be used to compute future loss of earnings in adjudication proceedings involving work injuries or accidental deaths.

FOREWORD

• •

The message of this book is simple: there is life without college. A four-year college degree was once the privilege of the moneyed minority. At the end of World War II, due in no small part to the passage of the G.I. Bill of Rights, which guaranteed a college education to any veteran who wanted it, college enrollment exploded. After that, encouraged by federal and state legislation guaranteeing loans and providing other entitlements, Americans continued to flock to colleges and universities in unprecedented numbers. It was a given that a college degree meant a better job, higher pay and, most of all, security. By 1992, over 21 percent of the adult population had earned degrees.

Today, the purely economic rationale for college is not as compelling as it once was. In recent years, the reality of an uncertain economy has dampened the ardor for higher education. College graduates are facing the bleakest job market since the Great Depression, and it is not expected to get any better soon.

Thousands of white-collar workers at all levels have been "outplaced." ("Outkicked" is more precise.) Hundreds of corporations, including the cream of the Fortune 500, have been eliminating professional and management positions held mainly by people with college degrees. The companies call it "downsizing," "restructuring," "reorganizing," or "reengineering." Employees call it "getting fired."

A word should be said about the cost of higher education today. Statistics published by the U.S. Department of Education tell us that the national average for tuition and room and board at a four-year private university is approximately $17,000 a year, not counting living expenses, books, special fees, and a host of other miscellaneous expenses. The price tag for a public university education has also crept up to a record figure, and the cost of an Ivy League university education has skyrocketed beyond reach of the average family. You can still get an education loan, but you will be mortgaging a part of your future income for a long time after graduation.

It is not the purpose of this book to try to influence the reader as to whether or not higher education should be pursued. This is a purely personal decision that must be based on personal goals. Obviously, for those wanting to enter certain professions, a degree is mandatory, and this book is not for those people. Additionally, a mere high school diploma will not qualify you for all occupations covered in these pages. Many jobs will require study in a technical or vocational school; some will demand graduation from a community or two-year college, while others will require serving an apprenticeship or undergoing a term of on-the-job training.

If you are just graduating from high school, not contemplating college, and looking for your first job; if you are now employed, but find your work either boring or financially unsatisfying; if you have been a victim of corporate shrinkage and don't know what to do next, this book will offer you some options and possibly point you to a new career that fulfills all of your desires and goals.

GOOD LUCK!

WHAT'S IN THIS BOOK

● ●

This book is divided into two sections: a job-hunting guide and a job finder.

Section One contains the job-hunting guide. Here you will learn the basic rules for getting the job you want, what personal attributes are necessary to beat the competition, and how to set up and use personal and business contacts to increase your chances of success.

Almost every job search begins with a resume. You will learn how to produce an effective resume and cover letters that get interviews. How you conduct yourself in an interview may determine whether you get a job offer. Included are tips on how to prepare for an interview and how to conduct yourself to enhance your chances of success.

The last part of this first section consists of a chapter on the best jobs for the future. What skills will be in demand? In what fields will the jobs occur, what will they pay, and how can you prepare yourself for them? Projections obtained from government and private sources are shown, offering readers the opportunity to prepare themselves for the career opportunities of the future.

Section Two, which begins with the heading "Job Finder" on the Contents page, consists of descriptions of 78 occupations that do not require a four-year college degree. This series of career clusters, or alphabetical listings of jobs relating to a particular field or industry, is intended to help those who have an interest in a specific field of work but who are not sure just what opportunities are open in that field. Or, you may first want to browse through the entire book to get an idea of what occupations are available to you in general.

Information about each occupation is divided into four categories: Job Description, Qualifications, Income and Advancement, and Where to Get More Information.

JOB DESCRIPTION. This section explains what workers do on the job, the tools and equipment they use, the amount of supervision they require, and the end products or services of their efforts.

Duties and responsibilities involved in each job usually vary by industry, the size of the employer, and the geographical location of the job. Job applicants with little formal education or training will probably start as trainees or apprentices. Advancement in responsibility and income comes with further education, training, and experience.

QUALIFICATIONS. Here you will learn what training and education are necessary for each occupation and where they may be acquired. Training is offered by high schools, colleges, postsecondary vocational schools (public and private), the Armed Forces, and employers, through classes, apprenticeships, and work-study programs. The kind of training you get often determines the level at which you enter an occupation and how quickly you advance.

In addition to formal training, employers look for people with certain personal characteristics, such as a positive attitude, self-confidence, and good work habits. Reading, writing, and communication skills are important in practically every job, as is the ability to get along with people. Many positions require mechanical aptitude, manual dexterity, mathematical skills, and the ability to work as part of a team. In addition, some occupations require applicants to pass an examination to obtain a certificate or license.

INCOME AND ADVANCEMENT. This section provides the most recent available data on earnings for each occupation. Methods of determining income vary. Some workers are paid an annual salary. Others are paid by the hour, or are paid a piece rate for each item they produce. Some receive commissions based on a percentage of what they sell. Workers may be paid a combination of salary or hourly wage plus bonus or tips. Keep in mind that whatever method an employer uses to compensate its employees, most workers also receive benefits such as paid vacations and holidays, health insurance, and pensions. Some also get profit-sharing, savings plans, tuition assistance, and bonuses. In many occupations, workers also may receive discounts on merchandise, meals and housing, reduced travel fares, expense accounts, childcare services, and the use of a company car.

Income projections are extracted from information provided by the latest available data from the U.S. Bureau of Labor Statistics and other sources. It should be noted that due to the delay between the time these statistics are gathered and the time they are published, they may be out of date and should be considered only as a rough guide, subject to change. In addition, earnings vary according to the geographical location and the size of the employer, the amount of education and training needed, and the technical skills required for the work. Current earnings information may be obtained by contacting the sources listed at the end of each occupation description.

WHERE TO GET MORE INFORMATION. The names and addresses of organizations listed at the end of each occupational chapter represent a wide variety of sources: trade associations, professional societies, labor unions, business firms, government agencies, and educational institutions. Most will provide free or inexpensive career material. In addition, many public libraries offer career information and can direct you to helpful books and periodicals.

Personal career counseling services are available at high school guidance offices, college placement departments, private vocational and technical school placement offices, vocational rehabilitation agencies, private career counseling services, and state employment service offices.

10 RULES FOR FINDING THE JOB YOU WANT

· ·

Rule 1: Job Hunting Is a Full-Time Occupation.

When you're unemployed the only thing that disappears faster than money is time, and the amount of time you spend actively looking for a job will determine how fast you will find one. Looking for a job is a full-time job. If you work at it part-time, you can't expect results. This means getting up early enough to start your search by 8:30 or 9:00 A.M. and not quitting until 4:00 or 5:00 P.M. every business day.

You have a lot of work to do every day: calling prospective employers, visiting employment agencies, writing and revising your resume, following up on letters and interviews, researching, networking, and lots more. An eight-hour day consists of only 480 minutes. Every minute wasted delays your getting a job and a paycheck. You will need willpower and discipline to keep yourself on the right track. Daytime television, household chores, shopping, and daydreaming are out for the duration.

The best way to take charge of your time is to organize your daily activities. For example, write a "things-to-do" list. Plan to answer appropriate "help-wanted" advertisements in your daily newspaper; visit the library to research books and articles on job hunting, and to consult directories for companies to contact; register with employment agencies; visit the local office of the state employment service; and network with your relatives, friends, and acquaintances. As your job search progresses, you will find that you will have little spare time on your hands, and that's the way it should be.

When an interview appears to go well, or when a job offer seems imminent, don't stop looking. Your search is not over until you report for work. Being busy is the best antidote for discouragement. Keeping your days filled with productive job-hunting activities will also help you cope with the stress and uncertainty associated with being unemployed.

Rule 2: Show Self-Confidence and Enthusiasm.

There are more agreeable ways to spend your time than hunting for a job. It's a challenging experience, physically and emotionally. Your ego will be assailed, and your self-assurance battered, at the hands of seemingly indifferent people. Idle hours spent in waiting rooms, cavalier treatment at the hands of some interviewers, and frequent rejection do not engender confidence. Unless luck favors you with a quick job offer, you will probably be in for your share of disappointments. No one ever said job hunting was easy, but the worst thing you can do when meeting prospective employers is to allow your frustration to show.

Enthusiasm is a key that can open locked doors. No great accomplishment was ever achieved without it. In your competition with other job applicants, enthusiasm can often give you an edge even if you have less experience. Make every interviewer feel that you are ready, willing, and eager to go to work, and that you are confident that you can be a valuable asset to the organization.

Rule 3: Start Your Search by Using People.

It's called networking, and it's a powerful tool. Some people are reluctant to use their personal contacts to help them find a job. Pride, embarrassment, and an unwillingness to ask for favors are some of the reasons job hunters don't take advantage of one of the best sources of help.

Put your pride in your pocket. Use people. It's no disgrace to be out of work. Almost everyone has been in the same circumstances at one time or another.

The best way to organize a networking campaign is to make three separate lists of the people you know. The first is people you have met in your work—for example, former employers, members of business or professional associations, previous co-workers, customers, and suppliers of former employers.

Your second list should include everyone who has ever provided you with a personal service: your accountant, stockbroker, attorney, insurance agent, doctor or dentist, banker, or clergyman.

For your third list, consider friends, acquaintances, former teachers, ex-roommates, alumni associations, school placement counselors, local politicians, former fellow students, school board members, and local merchants.

Each person you turn to for help has a sphere of influence, and the more people who are looking out for your interests, the better chance you have of landing the job you want.

Rule 4: Write a Resume That Sells.

Every job search begins with a resume. An effective resume is more than just a fact sheet; it is a selling tool that should be designed to get and hold the attention of the reader.

Resumes should always be typed or reproduced on good-quality white paper, never more or less than $8\frac{1}{2}$ inches wide and 11 inches long. You should allow at least $1\frac{1}{2}$ inches for left and right margins and double space between paragraphs. Limit your resume to one page, if possible; never make it more than two pages long.

Begin by assembling information about yourself. The following information should appear on your resume:

- Current address and phone number. If you are out of your home during business hours, try to give the phone number of a friend or relative, or, if that's not possible, use an answering machine, or subscribe to an answering service.

- Job sought or career objective.

- Education: the name and location of the school; years you attended; the diploma, certificate, or degree you earned; and what courses you took.

- Experience (paid and volunteer), dates of employment, names and full addresses of companies, title of each job, and your duties and responsibilities. Describe your contributions to employers. If you improved productivity, reduced costs, headed a project, increased sales, or improved efficiency objective, describe your achievements.

- Your experience with tools, machinery, computers, and office equipment. Include special skills such as languages, technical know-how, or mechanical ability.

The following information should *not* appear in your resume:

- Past or present salary (should be saved for the interview).

- Reasons for leaving a job.

- Negative or embarrassing information.

- Reference to religion, race, color, national origin.

- Height, weight, physical condition (unless you are applying for a job as a model or a bouncer).

- Personal information relating to marriage and children.

After writing the first draft, proofread it carefully for sense, grammar, punctuation, and sentence structure. Show your resume to someone else for an objective review. Then have a third person proofread it again.

Rule 5: Write an Intriguing Cover Letter.

Whenever you send a resume to a potential employer, attach a cover letter that will capture his or her attention. The purpose of a cover letter is to personalize your resume. It should feature a few highlights of your experience and background relating to the specific position you are seeking. It should explain how your employment will benefit the company, and it should ask for an interview. Here is what an effective cover letter should include:

Salutation. Each cover letter should be addressed by name to the person who can hire you. Call the company to obtain the correct name and title of the individual you want to reach, and be sure to spell the name correctly.

First paragraph. Explain why you are sending your resume, that is, whether you are responding to a help-wanted advertisement, writing on someone's recommendation, or submitting your qualifications for any current or future openings.

Body. Write a short paragraph briefly describing your qualifications. Follow this with a list of two or three specific accomplishments that relate to the particular job for which you are applying. Keep your letter short and to the point. Do not attempt to cram the entire contents of your resume into the letter.

Closing. Ask for an interview. Avoid the use of wimpy statements such as "Thank you for your consideration" or "I hope to hear from you soon." Notify the reader that you will call for an appointment in a few days, and be sure to include your phone number. End with "Sincerely yours," leave three or four lines of space, type your name, and be sure to sign it.

Rule 6: Prepare for the Interview.

If there is one key requirement for a successful interview, it's preparation. When you are talking to an interviewer, nothing is more depressing than the feeling of having left your brains at home. Do your homework; educate yourself about the company or organization in which you are seeking employment.

You can find information about companies at your public library. If the company is publicly owned, i.e., one whose stock is listed on any of the financial exchanges, you can call directly and request a copy of their latest financial statement. The statement will contain all you need to know about the firm.

Here are some ways to make a good showing at an interview.

- Offer a firm but less than bone-crushing handshake when entering the office.

- Don't mumble. Speak clearly and enunciate your words.

- Smile frequently.

- Be enthusiastic and upbeat in discussing your background and experience.

- The line between self-confidence and bragging is slim. Don't step over it.

- You should have nothing in your mouth except your tongue and teeth. Don't chew gum or smoke.

- Maintain your poise. Act self-assured but not cocky.

- Take it easy on perfume or cologne. Many people are allergic to them.

- Never criticize a former employer. It's in bad taste and can work against you.

- Never beg for a job. It makes interviewers uncomfortable and can be self-destructive.

- Avoid "yes" or "no" answers. Respond to all questions fully by giving all information requested, but know when to shut your mouth. Don't answer any questions you haven't been asked. Applicants have been known to talk their way into a job and out of it in the same breath.

- Do not whine. Keep all conversation to job-related subjects. Talking about personal problems is counterproductive.

- Don't overstay your welcome. When the interview is over, thank your interviewer for his or her interest and courtesy, and quit while you're ahead.

- When you get home from the interview, write a "thank you" letter. In it, express your appreciation for the interviewer's time, state that you feel that you can be an asset to the organization, offer to provide further information and references, and convey the hope that you will be favorably considered for the position.

Rule 7: Explore the "Hidden" Job Market.

A large percentage of job openings never go public. Statistics show that approximately 75 percent of all job openings are filled without benefit of advertising or the services of employment agencies. The only way to ferret out these jobs is to contact the firms directly.

The way to tap this hidden job market is to select the firms you want to reach and send a copy of your resume accompanied by a cover letter to the head of the appropriate department. Do not direct your letter to the personnel manager. Personnel is often the last to know of a job opening.

How do you find potential employers? There are directories published that list almost every company, organization, association, and institution in America. They are available to you at public libraries. Consult the reference librarian for the directory that lists the kind of companies or organizations you are looking for.

These publications contain detailed information about each listed firm, including address, telephone and fax numbers, size, number of employees, location of plants and offices, names of parent or subsidiary companies, names and titles of executives and department managers, products or services, annual sales volume, and more.

Before you contact the designated individual in the company you have chosen, call to confirm that he or she is still there in the same position. Directories are compiled months in advance of their publication, and personnel changes often occur in the interim.

If you have not heard anything within a week after you sent your cover letter and resume, follow up with a telephone call. Try to call before 8:00 A.M. or after 5:00 P.M. Most supervisors arrive earlier and leave later than other workers, and you want to avoid reaching secretaries or assistants who won't put you through without a lot of questions. When you do get your party, don't apologize for the call. Go right into your pitch. "Hello, Ms. Anderson, this is Mary Jones. I'm following up on the letter and resume I sent to you April 9th." Don't stop and wait for a response. Keep talking. "If you recall, I was a medical laboratory assistant for the Forest Hills Medical Center. If you could spare a few minutes, I would like to stop in and talk to you about my background and education." This approach will not always get you an immediate interview, but if you follow up on all your resumes, you are bound to get some invitations for an interview.

Rule 8: Organize a Follow-Up System.

After a few weeks of answering help-wanted ads, making countless phone calls, and arranging interviews, you will have been exposed to numerous names, addresses, and telephone numbers of people and companies. Your cover letters and resumes will be all over town, and you will have discussed qualifications, salaries, benefits, and other vital information for a wide variety of jobs.

Unless you systematically organize and record all this information and the details of your many interviews on a daily basis, you will not be able to conduct a logical and successful job-hunting campaign.

Get a supply of 5×8-inch index cards. (The standard 3×5-inch cards are too small for all the information you will have to write on them.) Use a separate card for each company, employment agency, or network contact. On the card write the full names, addresses, and telephone numbers of the companies and individuals you communicate with. When you send a resume or letter, write the date you sent it and any response you receive. Use the individual cards to record summaries of any interviews or telephone conversations. Include salary data, impressions of the company and interviewer, an assessment of the interview, and any other pertinent data. Clip the card to any letters, business cards, company literature, or annual reports you receive.

The reasons for this system are obvious. Should you be contacted by a prospective employer, you will have the necessary information at your fingertips and will not have to depend on vague memories of facts and figures when you need them in a hurry.

Rule 9: Get Your First Job Offer.

The age-old question of how to get a job without experience, and how to get experience without a job, is still largely unanswered.

Even so, millions of new workers do enter the job force each year. Of course, not everyone gets the kind of job that he or she wants, and many applicants remain unhired for long periods. But with perseverance, determination, the right attitude, and hard work, you can beat the statistics.

As you prepare to look for your first full-time job, you may think that you are about to make the most important decision of your life. You are not. It is this attitude that causes beginners to over-analyze every prospective employer and every job offer while they look for the "right" job offering the "right" salary, benefits, and future. If you are perpetually fearful of accepting a job because you think it does not fulfill your every expectation, you will wind up looking far beyond a reasonable length of time, sacrificing valuable experience and income.

You will probably have several jobs, and perhaps even several careers, in your working lifetime, each change becoming more important to your career. You have only two basic factors to consider in choosing your first job: (1) that it is in, or related to, the field you have chosen, and (2) that the company offers the opportunity to get the training and experience you need to advance.

Salary and benefits should be secondary at this stage of your career. Starting salaries are relatively low. Your first concern should be opportunity. If you have that, the money will follow. Many beginners lose excellent opportunities because they set a minimum salary at the wrong time.

As a first-time job hunter, you should use every available source of jobs and enlist the help of everyone you can. Register with local employment agencies, visit the nearest branch of your state employment service, and contact your high school guidance counselor or your college placement office. Most vocational and trade schools have placement services that may be helpful. Use your network of friends, teachers, relatives, and fellow students; and thoroughly read the classified help-wanted section of your daily newspaper.

Rule 10: Look Your Best.

Success in landing a job depends to a great extent on your ability to convey a positive image. A large part of that image is your attire.

First impressions are made in the first minute or two of an interview, and how you look may well turn out to be a deciding factor in getting hired. This has nothing to do with your resemblance to Kevin Costner or Julia Roberts, but it does have to do with the clothes you wear and how you wear them.

You don't have to spend next month's rent money on your job-hunting wardrobe, but your clothes should be pressed and clean. What you wear depends on what kind of job you are seeking. If you're looking for a job as an automobile mechanic, no one expects you to appear in a three-piece, pinstriped suit and a tie. On the other hand, you don't want to show up for a job at a bank wearing jeans and western boots. For a job in a business office, a man should wear a dark suit, light-color shirt, conservative tie, and leather shoes. Women have more of a choice. They can wear jackets and skirts or suits. Overpowering cologne or perfume is not recommended for either men or women. For so-called blue-collar jobs in the trades, attire can be much more informal, but avoid jeans, T-shirts, scuffed basketball shoes, and garish jewelry.

In the eyes of an interviewer, you are what you wear, so use common sense. And always remember that neatness counts.

21 HOT JOBS FOR TOMORROW

• •

By the year 2005, employment in the United States will reach a record of 147.5 million jobs, an increase of 26 percent, according to a report published by the U.S. Bureau of Labor Statistics. An expanding economy is expected to increase the demand for products and services and create jobs in almost every field between now and the beginning of the twenty-first century. Where will these jobs exist?

Nearly four out of five jobs will be found in industries that provide services, with the two largest groups, health services and business services, accounting for the largest percentage of the growth. In fact, jobs for health technologists and technicians are expected to account for over half of all the new jobs in this group. Business and industry will require more technicians and related support personnel. This includes engineering and science technicians, computer specialists, aircraft pilots, air traffic controllers, broadcast technicians, and clinical laboratory technicians.

Other occupations that will experience growth include paralegals; construction workers; marketing and sales representatives; mechanics; installers and repairers; and travel, transportation, and material moving workers.

The following is a list of the 21 fastest growing jobs, as projected by the U.S. Department of Labor. These jobs are expected to experience growth of at least 25 percent over the next 10 years. They are listed by the predicted percentage of growth, with the highest listed first.

Paralegals
Projected Growth Rate: 86%

Employment is expected to grow much faster than average as law firms and other employers of legal workers need trained personnel to prepare and handle the many documents and details for attorneys in a variety of occupational settings.

Correction officers
Projected Growth Rate: 70%

As correctional facilities expand and additional officers are hired to supervise and counsel the growing number of inmates, employment is expected to increase markedly. Rapid growth and replacement needs will mean favorable employment prospects.

Travel agents
Projected Growth Rate: 66%

Employment is expected to grow much faster than average due to the sharp increase in business and vacation travel.

Radiologic technologists
Projected Growth Rate: 63%

The development of improved diagnostic imaging equipment plus a continuing growth in the nation's aging population should increase demand for trained technologists.

Medical records technicians
Projected Growth Rate: 61%

Faster-than-average growth is projected due to the increasing demand for medical tests, treatments, and procedures and the need to scrutinize medical records by third-party payers, courts, and consumers.

EEG technologists   Projected Growth Rate: 54%

Employment is expected to grow much faster than average, reflecting the increased number of neurodiagnostic tests being performed. As the elderly population grows, it will require more medical care.

Flight attendants   Projected Growth Rate: 51%

As the number of airline passengers continues to increase, and as attendants retire, the air transportation industry will need to add new employees at an increased rate.

Restaurant and food   Projected Growth Rate: 46%
service managers

Population growth, rising personal incomes, and increased leisure time will continue to produce growth in the number of eating establishments and, therefore, of managers. People with training in restaurant or institutional food service management will have the best opportunities.

Nurses—registered   Projected Growth Rate: 42%

Much-faster-than-average growth is expected due to overall growth of health care and medical technology. Many job openings will also result from the need to replace experienced nurses who leave this large occupation.

Nurses—licensed practical   Projected Growth Rate: 42%

General demand and the long-term-care needs of a rapidly growing elderly population will require increasing numbers of LPNs into the twenty-first century.

Dental hygienists   Projected Growth Rate: 42%

Employment should grow much faster than average because of demand for dental care. Demand will arise from population growth, greater retention of natural teeth by middle-aged and elderly people, and rising incomes. Dentists are likely to hire more hygienists as their workloads increase.

Surgical technologists   Projected Growth Rate: 42%

Technological advances in medicine continue to increase the number of surgical procedures performed. Growth will be fastest in clinics and offices of physicians due to increased outpatient surgery. Most jobs, however, will be in hospitals.

Aircraft pilots   Projected Growth Rate: 35%

Air travel for business and pleasure will continue to increase, requiring the skills of a steady supply of pilots. Replacement for retiring pilots will continue to be a factor in airline hiring plans.

Securities and financial   Projected Growth Rate: 33%
sales representatives

Employment is expected to grow faster than average as economic growth, rising personal incomes, and greater inherited wealth increase the funds available for investment. Banks and other financial institutions will continue to offer an increasing array of financial services. Mature individuals with successful sales experience will enjoy opportunities in this field.

Automotive body repairers   Projected Growth Rate: 30%

Employment is expected to increase faster than average due to the rise in the number of motor vehicles. Opportunities should be best for those with formal training in automotive body repairs or mechanics.

Computer and office machine service technicians

Projected Growth Rate: 30%

Employment of computer repairers is expected to grow much faster than average as the amount of computer equipment in use increases. The need for repairers of other office machines will grow steadily as offices automation continues to expand.

Heating, air-conditioning, and refrigeration mechanics

Projected Growth Rate: 29%

Demand for new residential, commercial, and industrial climate control systems, as well as the need to maintain existing systems, should create very favorable job prospects over the next decade.

Bricklayers and stonemasons

Projected Growth Rate: 26%

Population and business growth is expected to create a need for new factories, schools, hospitals, offices, and other structures, and brick is increasingly used for decorative work and for building exteriors.

Clinical laboratory technologists and technicians

Projected Growth Rate: 26%

The fastest growth in this field is expected in independent medical laboratories. Rapid growth also is expected in the offices and clinics of physicians, as they continue to send laboratories a greater share of their testing.

Truck drivers   Projected Growth Rate: 26%

Job opportunities in this occupation should be plentiful because of
the growing demand for truck transportation services and the need
to replace drivers who leave the occupation.

Radio and television   Projected Growth Rate: 25%
announcers and newscasters

As new radio and television stations are licensed, and the number of
cable television systems continues to grow, opportunities in these
fields will become available. Radio stations are more inclined than
are television stations to hire beginners.

Growth of an occupation is only one reason for job opportunities. Most job vacancies occur to replace workers who, for one reason or another, move to other kinds of jobs or decide to change
careers. Some completely leave the job market to get further education or raise a family. Others go into business for themselves. Many
prefer early retirement, thereby creating openings. Occupations with
slower-than-average growth potential can still offer opportunities.

JOB FINDER

ADMINISTRATIVE, SUPPORT, AND CLERICAL

● ●

Administrative/Office Services Manager

Job Description

The center of every organization or business is its administrative office. The efficient operation of the modern office is due, in large measure, to the skills and ability of its administrative/office services manager.

Administrative office supervisors direct and coordinate support services, such as secretarial, payroll, conference planning, travel, information processing, mail, materials scheduling and distribution, reproduction, data processing, acquisition and maintenance of office equipment, and other necessary functions. They report to their mid-level counterparts, who, in turn, report to top-level executives.

Supervisory-level administrative managers directly oversee staffs involved in support services. They develop procedures to improve services, define and delegate office staff responsibilities, and coordinate the workflow and production.

They are often involved with the hiring and dismissal of employees, but generally have no rule in the formulation of personnel policies.

In small firms, one administrative services manager may oversee all support services. In larger organizations, each department or division will have a manager. Managers may also work as contract administrators, who direct the preparation, analysis, negotiation, and review of contracts related to the purchase of office equipment, supplies, and services.

Qualifications

Administrative services managers may advance through the ranks of an organization after several years of work experience in various administrative duties. Managers who oversee clerical and secretarial employees should be familiar with office procedures and equipment and have a working knowledge of word processing, communications, data processing, and record keeping.

Educational requirements vary widely. For supervisory-level administrative services managers of secretarial, mail room, and related support activities, many employers prefer an associate of arts degree from a two-year community college in business or management, or graduation from a business school.

To become an administrative/office services manager, you must be able to communicate and establish effective work relationships with people at all levels: managers, supervisors, professionals, clerks, and blue-collar workers. Managers should be detail-oriented and flexible, and possess the ability to cope with the stress of tight deadlines.

Income and Advancement

The median annual salary of administrative/office services managers is $35,000 to $40,000, with the highest-paid managers earning $50,000 or more.

They receive a range of fringe benefits such as vacation and sick leave, health and life insurance, and pension plans, among others, similar to those received by other management personnel.

Where to Get More Information

Academy of Administrative Management, 550 W. Jackson Blvd., Chicago, IL 60661.

Association of Records Managers and Administrators, 4200 Somerset Dr., Prairie Village, KS 66208.

Clerical Supervisor and Manager

Job Description

Organizations and businesses need effective administrative and clerical support to operate smoothly and efficiently. Coordinating this work and keeping it flowing unimpeded is the responsibility of clerical supervisors and managers.

Sometimes referred to as "office managers," clerical supervisors are responsible for administrative tasks that ensure their staff can work efficiently. Equipment and machinery used in their departments must be in good working order. If the computer system goes down or a photocopier malfunctions, they must try to find the problem and call in repair personnel.

The planning and supervision of their staff is a key function of the job. The supervisor must know the strengths and weaknesses of each member of the staff as well as the required level of quality and time allotted to each task. Supervisors must adjust assignments or perform the work themselves if the situation requires it.

Another part of the clerical supervisor's job is to conduct performance evaluations, recording them in the employee's personnel file. He or she may recommend a promotion or, if warranted, give advice on how to improve the worker's performance. Supervisors may suggest a transfer or dismissal if the situation does not improve.

Clerical supervisors and managers also interview prospective clerical employees and make recommendations regarding their hiring. When new workers arrive on the job, clerical supervisors and managers greet the new members of the staff and familiarize them with the daily routine of the workplace and the overall operation of the organization.

Supervisors act as the liaison between their clerical staff and other professional, technical, and managerial staff. They keep their superiors informed of their progress and alert their superiors to any potential problems. They also try to resolve interpersonal conflicts among the staff.

In organizations covered by union contracts, supervisors must know the provisions of labor-management agreements and run their departments accordingly. They may meet with union representatives to discuss work problems or grievances.

Qualifications

Most people enter this occupation from other occupations within the organization, very often from the ranks of those they subsequently supervise. To be promoted to a supervisory position, clerical or administrative support workers must first prove that they are capable of handling additional responsibility and have strong teamwork skills, determination, loyalty, poise, and confidence. They must also have the ability to organize and coordinate work efficiently, to set priorities, to give and follow orders, and to motivate others. Good working knowledge of the organization's computer system is an advantage.

Many employers also require some postsecondary training, such as a two-year associate degree from a community college or completion of a program at a vocational school.

Income and Advancement

Median annual earnings of full-time clerical supervisors are about $29,800, with the range being between $21,000 and $38,400. The top 10 percent earn more than $51,300. Supervisors who are willing and able to accept more responsibility can advance to higher management levels within the organization.

Where to Get More Information

State employment services can provide information about earnings, hours, and employment in this and other clerical jobs.

Computer Operator

Job Description

Computers are everywhere, and their numbers are increasing by leaps and bounds. The job of the computer operator is to see that the machines are used as efficiently as possible. Duties vary with the size of the installation and the type of equipment used. In organizations with small computer systems, for example, computer operators run both the computer and all the peripheral equipment, such as printers, disk drives, and tape readers. In large computer installations, computer operators specialize in console operation while periperal-equipment operators run the related devices.

Working from operating instructions prepared by programmers and information managers, computer operators set controls on the computer and peripheral devices required to run a particular job. They load the equipment with tapes, disks, and paper as needed. While the computer is running—which may be 24 hours a day for large computers—operators monitor the console and respond to operating and computer messages. If an error message occurs, operators must locate the problem and solve it or terminate the program.

As the trend toward networking—making connections between computers—accelerates, a growing number of these workers are operating personal computers (PCs). More and more establishments are realizing the need to connect all their computers in order to enhance productivity. In many offices, factories, and other work settings, PCs serve as the center of such networks, often referred to as local area networks (LANs) or multiuser systems. Computer operators may be required to work evening or night shifts and weekends. Shift assignments generally are made on the basis of seniority.

Qualifications

Previous training or work experience is generally necessary to land an operator job in many organizations. Employers look for specific, hands-on experience on the type of equipment and related operating systems that they use. Although some of the largest firms may require a bachelor's degree in computer science or data processing, most firms are willing to provide informal training because their computer systems are not as expensive nor downtime as costly as in larger installations. In these smaller shops, education may be substituted for experience to some extent. A high school diploma and some business or technical school training are usually required for entry-level positions. Workers usually receive some on-the-job training to become acquainted with their employer's equipment and routines. The length of training varies with the job and the experience of the operator. Computer operators must be able to communicate well in order to work effectively with programmers and each other and also must be able to work independently because they have little or no supervision. Operators may advance to supervisory jobs.

Income and Advancement

Earnings for full-time computer operators range from about $16,000 to more than $38,700 per year, depending on the geographic location, the size of the organization, and the experience of the operator.

Through on-the-job experience and additional formal education, some operators can advance to jobs as programmers and operations analysts.

Where to Get More Information

For information about work opportunities in computer operations, contact firms that make heavy use of computers, such as banks, insurance firms, manufacturing companies, universities, and data processing service organizations. The local office of the state employment service can supply information about employment and training opportunities.

Court Reporter and Stenographer

Job Description

Written accounts of spoken words are necessary for correspondence, records, and legal documents. Speeches, conversations, legal proceedings, meetings, or other events are recorded verbatim by stenographers and court reporters.

Stenographers and stenotype operators take dictation and then transcribe their notes on a typewriter or word processor. They may take shorthand or use a stenotype machine, which prints shorthand symbols. General stenographers take routine dictation, whereas highly skilled stenographers take more difficult dictation. They may sit in on staff meetings and provide word-for-word records or summary reports of the proceedings. Some stenographers take dictation in foreign languages; others work as public stenographers serving traveling business people and others.

Technical stenographers must know medical, legal, and engineering or scientific terminology. Medical transcriptionists, for example, listen to doctors' audio tapes and, using a typewriter or word processor, transcribe what they hear into the proper format.

Court reporters record all statements made in official proceedings and trials. They take down all statements at speeds of 200 words per minute or more and present their records as official transcripts. Many court reporters do freelance work recording depositions for attorneys, proceeding of meetings and conventions, and other private activities. Others record the proceedings in the U.S. Congress, in state and local governing bodies, and in government agencies at all levels.

Some reporters dictate proceedings on magnetic tapes that a typist can transcribe later. Most of them use stenotype machines that print phonetic symbols on computer tapes or disks. These are then loaded on a computer that prints the symbols in English. This is called "computer-aided transcription." Stenotype machines that are directly linked to the computer are used for "real-time captioning";

that is, as the reporter types the symbols, the computer transcribes them instantly. This process is used in closed captioning for the deaf or hearing-impaired on television, in courts, or in meetings.

Qualifications

Stenographic skills are taught in high schools, vocational schools, and business schools. Court reporting programs are offered in two-year community and junior colleges and in private schools, which also teach computer-aided transcription. Employers hire high school graduates and usually have no preference among the many different shorthand methods. For court reporters, however, the preference is for stenotype, not only because reporters can write faster, but also because they can feed stenotype notes to a computer for high-speed transmission. Although requirements vary in private firms, applicants with the best speed and accuracy will received first consideration in hiring. Many court reporting jobs require more than 225 words of dictation per minute.

Some states require each court reporter to be a Certified Court Reporter (CCR). The National Court Reporters Association confers the designation Registered Professional Reporter (RPR) upon those who pass a two-part examination and participate in continuing education programs. The RPR designation is recognized as a mark of excellence in the profession.

Income and Advancement

Salaries for general stenographers in private industry range from $16,000 to $25,000 per year. Technical and medical stenographers usually earn more. Earnings depend on speed, education, experience, and geographic location. Stenographers can advance to secretaries or administrative assistants and, with the necessary education, can become court reporters.

Court reporters earn from $30,000 to $75,000 a year and more. During court trials, attorneys and other interested parties may require additional copies of transcripts, for which court reporters charge a per-page fee. Depending upon the length and complexity of the trial, this can add substantially to court reporters' incomes. Many court reporters are employed by court reporting firms. Others work freelance or open their own firms, hiring other reporters for assignments.

Where to Get More Information

American Association for Medical Transcriptionists, P.O. Box 576187, Modesto, CA 95357.

National Court Reporters Association, 8224 Old Courthouse Rd., Vienna, VA 22182.

Credit Clerk and Authorizer

Job Description

Give credit where credit is due. That is the job of credit clerks and credit authorizers. When you apply for credit—to buy a home, furniture and appliances, or a car, or to get a credit card—a credit clerk or authorizer reviews your credit history and obtains the information needed to determine whether credit will be extended and how much. Credit clerks contact applicants, credit bureaus, and other sources for information. Credit authorizers refer to credit reports to decide whether to approve a customer's credit card purchase.

In credit bureaus, these workers are often called credit investigators or reporters. In banks and other financial institutions, they process loan and credit applications. Some verify employment and financial information of credit card applicants.

Credit authorizers approve charges against customers' existing accounts. Charges are usually approved by computer. However, when accounts are past due, overextended, invalid, or show any change in residence, salespersons refer transactions to central office credit authorizers who evaluate the customers's credit records and payment histories and quickly decide whether to approve new charges.

Almost three-fourths of credit clerks and authorizers are employed in banks and other financial institutions, and about 10 percent are in wholesale and retail trade. The rest work for business services, such as credit reporting and collection agencies, and computer or data processing services.

Qualifications

No specific training is needed for beginning positions. New employees are generally trained on the job, working under close supervision of experienced workers. Some also take courses in credit offered by banking and credit associations and public and private vocational schools. Positions involve a substantial amount of telephone contact, so good communications skills are necessary. Organizational skills and the ability to handle details are also very important.

Income and Advancement

Earnings range from $17,000 to $30,000 per year, depending on the experience of the worker and the size and geographical location of the employer company. Credit clerks and authorizers can advance to loan or credit department supervisor, underwriter, or management. For management positions, employers prefer applicants with at least some business or management courses at a community college or junior college, or one or more years at a regular college or university.

Where to Get More Information

Information about local job opportunities in the credit field may be obtained from retail stores, banks, and credit reporting agencies.

Additional information may be obtained by contacting:

National Association of Credit Management (NACM), and Credit Research Foundation (the education and research affiliate of NACM), 8815 Centre Park Dr., Columbia, MD 21045.

Employment Interviewer

Job Description

Almost everyone, at one time or another, has had to turn to an employment interviewer for help. Sometimes known as personnel consultants, employment agents, recruiters, human resources specialists, employment brokers, or head hunters, they have two main functions: to help jobseekers find employment and help employers find qualified staff.

Working largely in private personnel supply firms or state employment security offices (also known as job or employment service centers), employment interviewers act as brokers, bringing together the best combination of applicant and job.

Private industry employment interviewers are primarily salespersons. Counselors try to "sell" qualified job applicants to many different companies. They will call companies that have never been clients with the aim of filling their employment needs.

Employers generally pay private employment agencies for finding them workers. The employer places a "job order" with the agency, describing the opening and listing requirements, such as education, credentials, and experience. Job seekers are asked to fill out applications or present resumes that detail their education, experience, and other qualifications. The interviewer then reviews the job order and the job seeker's qualifications to determine the best possible match. Counselors offer tips on personal appearance, suggestions on presenting a positive picture of oneself, background on the company with which an interview is arranged, and recommendations about interviewing techniques. Many firms specialize in placing applicants in particular kinds of jobs—for example, secretarial, word processing, engineering, accounting, law, or health. Counselors in such firms usually have experience in the field into which they are placing applicants.

Some interviewers work in temporary help services. These companies send out their own employees to firms that need temporary help.

The duties of employment interviewers in state job service centers are somewhat different because applicants may lack marketable skills. Here, applicants present resumes and fill out forms that ask for education, job history, skills, awards, certificates, and licenses. The employment interviewer then tries to match these qualifications with the type of job sought and salary range desired. Some applicants are hindered by such problems as poor English language skills, no high school diploma, a history of drug or alcohol dependency, or a prison record. The amount and nature of special help for such applicants vary from state to state.

Three out of five employment interviewers work for private employment firms or temporary help services. Most of the rest work for state employment security agencies.

Qualifications

There are no specific educational requirements for a job as an employment interviewer. Firms that place highly trained individuals, such as accountants, lawyers, engineers, physicians, or managers, prefer their interviewers to have some training or experience in the field. Sales ability is a key factor for success in the private sector.

Desirable qualifications for employment interviewers include good communications skills, a desire to help people, and office skills. A friendly manner is an asset because personal interaction is a large part of this occupation. Because computers are increasingly used as a tool by employment interviewers, knowledge of computers is helpful.

Income and Advancement

Because the basis for compensation varies, workers in personnel supply firms generally are paid on a commission basis, whereas those in temporary help services receive a salary. Commission earnings depend on how much business is brought in and how many placements are made. Those working strictly on a commission basis are usually paid between 30 and 45 percent of what he or she bills the client, although this figure varies widely from firm to firm. Some work on salary plus commission, guaranteeing these workers security through slow times while the commission provides the incentive and opportunity for higher earnings.

According to limited data available, average earnings of interviewers or counselors in personnel supply and temporary help services range from about $17,000 to $25,000 a year. Some earn considerably more. Counselors who place professional workers or higher-level management personnel can earn from $30,000 to $75,000 a year and more.

Where to Get More Information

National Association of Personnel Consultants, 3133 Mt. Vernon Ave., Alexandria, VA 22305.

National Association of Temporary Services, 119 S. Saint Asaph St., Alexandria, VA 22314.

Library Technician

Job Description

Library technicians assist librarians in the performance of their duties. They help them acquire, prepare, and organize books, and help users find materials and information. Technicians assist the public in the use of catalogs, direct them to standard references, organize and maintain periodicals, perform routine cataloging and coding of library materials, verify information, retrieve information from computer databases, and supervise other support staff.

Some library technicians operate audiovisual equipment and assist library users with microfilm or microfiche readers. They also help teachers get instructional materials and assist students with special assignments. Some work in special libraries maintained by government agencies, corporations, law firms, advertising agencies, museums, professional societies, medical centers, and research laboratories.

Most library technicians work in school, academic, or public libraries. Some work in hospitals and religious organizations.

Qualifications

Training requirements for library technicians vary widely, ranging from a high school diploma to training as a library technician. Employers may hire individuals with work experience or other training, or they may train inexperienced workers on the job.

Some two-year colleges offer an associate of arts degree in library technology. Students learn about library organization and operation and how to order, process, catalog, locate, and circulate library materials, and work with library automation.

Income and Advancement

Salaries for library technicians vary widely, depending on the type of library and its geographic location. They range from $18,000 to $24,000 a year.

Where to Get More Information

Council on Library/Media Technicians, P.O. Box 951, Oxon Hill, MD 20750.

American Library Association, Office for Library Personnel Resources, 50 East Huron St., Chicago, IL 60611.

Office of Educational Research and Improvement, Library Programs, Library Development Staff, U.S. Department of Education, 555 New Jersey Ave., NW, Washington, DC 20208.

Paralegal

Job Description

You don't need a law degree to do certain kinds of legal work. Lawyers are often assisted by paralegals or "legal assistants," who perform many of the same tasks as lawyers.

Paralegals work directly under the supervision of lawyers. While the lawyer assumes responsibility for the paralegal's work, a paralegal is often allowed to perform all the functions of a lawyer other than accepting clients, setting legal fees, giving legal advice, or presenting a case in court.

Paralegals generally do background work for lawyers. To help prepare a case for trial, a paralegal investigates the facts of the case to make sure that all relevant information is uncovered. Paralegals may conduct research to identify the appropriate laws, judicial decisions, legal articles, and other material that will be used to determine whether the client has a good case. Paralegals may prepare a written report that is used to decide how the case should be handled, and they may assist in the preparation of legal arguments, draft pleadings to be filed with court, obtain affidavits, and assist the attorney during the trial. They also may keep files of all documents and correspondence important to the case.

Besides litigation, they also work in such areas as bankruptcy, corporate law, criminal law, employee benefits, patent and copyright law, and real estate. They help draft such documents as contracts, mortgages, separation agreements, and trust instruments. They may also help prepare tax returns and plan estates.

Paralegals who work for corporations help attorneys with such matters as employee contracts, shareholder agreements, stock option plans, and employee benefit plans. They may help prepare and file annual financial reports, maintain corporate minute books and resolutions, and help secure loans for the corporation.

A growing number of paralegals use computers in their work. Computer software programs are used to search legal literature stored in the computer and identify legal texts relevant to a specific subject.

Private law firms employ the vast majority of paralegals. Most of the remainder work for various levels of government as well as banks, real estate development companies, and insurance companies.

Qualifications

Employers generally require formal paralegal training. Some employers, however, prefer to train their paralegals on the job, promoting experienced legal secretaries. Other entrants have experience in a technical field that is useful to law firms, such as a background in tax preparation for tax and estate practice, or nursing or health administration for personal injury practice.

Formal paralegal training programs are offered by community and junior colleges, business schools, and proprietary schools. Most paralegal programs are completed in two years. Programs typically include a combination of general courses on such subjects as the law and legal research techniques, and courses that cover specialized areas of the law, such as real estate planning and probate, litigation, family law, contracts, and criminal law.

Many paralegal training programs include an internship in which students gain practical experience by working for several months in a law office, corporate legal department, or government agency. Experience gained in internships is an asset for those seeking a job after graduation. Paralegals must have good research and investigative skills, and be familiar with the operation and applications of computers in legal research and litigation support.

Income and Advancement

Earnings of paralegals vary greatly. Salaries depend on the education, training, and experience the paralegal brings to the job; the type and size of employer company; and the geographic location of the job.

Starting salaries of paralegals average about $23,400 a year, while those with experience earn from about $24,800 to $30,000 and more. In addition to a salary, many paralegals receive an annual bonus, plus life and health insurance benefits and contributions toward a retirement plan.

Experienced paralegals usually are given progressively more responsible duties and less supervision. In large law firms, corporate legal departments, and government agencies, experienced paralegals may supervise other paralegals and clerical staff. Advancement opportunities include promotion to managerial and other law-related positions within the firm or corporate legal department.

Where to Get More Information

Standing Committee on Legal Assistants, American Bar Association, 750 North Lake Shore Dr., Chicago, IL 60611.

National Association of Legal Assistants, Inc., 160 S. Main St., Tulsa, OK 74119.

National Federation of Paralegal Associations, P.O. Box 33108, Kansas City, MO 64114.

American Association for Paralegal Education, P.O. Box 40244, Overland Park, KS 66204.

Postal Clerk and Mail Carrier

Job Description

"Neither rain nor snow, nor gloom of night, shall stay these couriers from their appointed rounds." This is the motto of the U.S. Postal Service. The 792,000 postal workers employed by the postal service strive daily to make those words come true.

Clerks and carriers are distinguished by the type of work they do. Clerks are usually classified by the mail-processing function they perform, whereas carriers are classified by their type of route.

About 350 mail-processing centers service post offices, staffed primarily by postal clerks, in surrounding areas. Some clerks, referred to as mail handlers, unload the sacks of incoming mail; separate letters, parcel post, magazines, and newspapers; and transport these to the appropriate sorting and processing area. After letters have been put through stamp-canceling machines, they are taken to other workrooms to be sorted according to destination. Clerks operating electronic letter-sorting machines punch keys corresponding to the zip code of the local post office to which each letter will be delivered. The machine then drops the letters into the proper slots.

A growing proportion of clerks operate optical character readers (OCRs) and bar code sorters, machines that can "read" the address and sort a letter according to the code printed on the envelope. Finally, the mail is sent to local post offices for sorting according to delivery route, then delivered. At local post offices, clerks provide retail services, such as the selling of stamps and money orders and the weighing of packages. They also register, certify, and insure mail and answer questions about rates, post office boxes, mailing restrictions, and other postal matters.

Once the mail has been processed and sorted, it is ready to be delivered by mail carriers, who cover the route by foot or by vehicle.

Qualifications

Postal clerks and mail carriers must be U.S. citizens or have been granted permanent resident-alien status. They must be 18 years old, or 16 if they have a high school diploma. Qualification is based on a written examination.

Applicants should apply at the post office or mail-processing center where they wish to work in order to determine when an exam will be given. Their names are listed in order of their examination scores. Extra points are added to the score of honorably discharged veterans.

A good memory, good coordination, and the ability to read rapidly and accurately are important.

Income and Advancement

According to the most recent information, beginning full-time carriers and postal clerks earn $23,737 a year, which rises to $33,952 after $12^1/_2$ years of service. A supplement is paid for those working between 6:00 P.M. and 6:00 A.M. Those working part-time flexible schedules begin at $11.81 an hour and, based on the number of years of service, increase their pay to $16.91 an hour.

Most of these workers belong to one of four unions: American Postal Workers Union, National Association of Letter Carriers, National Postal Mail Handlers Union, and National Rural Letter Carriers Association.

Where to Get More Information

Local post offices and state employment service offices can supply details about entrance examinations and specific employment opportunities for postal clerks and mail carriers.

Secretary

Job Description

In Latin, the word *secretary* means "keeper of the secrets." Once hired for their skills in shorthand and typing, secretaries now have duties much more diverse. Referred to by many employers as administrative assistants, they perform a wide variety of duties that are necessary to run and maintain an organization's efficiency. These duties depend upon their level of responsibility and the type of firm in which they are employed.

"Take a letter, Ms. Jones" is a statement not often heard in modern offices. In today's automated environment, secretaries seldom take dictation in notebooks. They often operate complex electronic equipment. They may use computers to run spreadsheets, database management, desktop publishing, and word processing programs. They contact clients, make travel arrangements, provide information to callers, and assist executives in a wide range of tasks.

Executive secretaries may handle more complex duties, such as conducting research, preparing reports, and supervising and training clerical employees.

Secretaries with specialized knowledge of technical terms are employed by attorneys, physicians, engineers, and scientists.

About one-half of all secretaries are employed in firms providing services, ranging from education and health to legal and business services. Others work in a variety of organizations, such as banking, retail trade, manufacturing, communications, transportation, and finance as well as federal, state, and local government agencies.

Qualifications

A high school diploma is a prerequisite, providing that the applicant has basic office skills. Employers require secretaries to be proficient in spelling, punctuation, grammar, and oral communications. Shorthand is necessary for some positions. These skills can be acquired through formal training at high school vocational education programs or in one- or two-year programs in secretarial science offered by business schools, technical schools, and community colleges. Specialized programs are available for those desiring to become legal or medical secretaries, or office automation specialists.

Income and Advancement

Salaries for secretaries depend on skills, experience, and geographical location. They range from $20,000 to $32,000 and more. Salaries also vary by industry and tend to be higher in transportation, legal services, and public utilities. Experienced executive secretaries working for high-level corporate executives can earn from $40,000 to $50,000, plus bonuses.

Advancement for secretaries is generally made through promotion to more responsible secretarial or administrative positions. Those who expand their knowledge of their firm's operations may be promoted to other clerical supervisor or office manager positions. Secretaries with word processing skills can advance to word processing trainers, supervisors, or managers within their own firms or in word processing service bureaus. They are often employed with manufacturers of computer equipment as instructors or sales representatives.

Where to Get More Information

Professional Secretaries International, 10502 N.W. Ambassador Dr., Kansas City, MO 64195.

National Association of Legal Secretaries, 2250 East 73rd St., Tulsa, OK 74136.

COMMUNICATIONS AND VISUAL ARTS

• •

Designer

Job Description

Consumers look for products that not only serve the purpose for which they were intended but are visually pleasing as well. To accomplish this, designers use their training and skills to organize and design products that are eye-catching as well as functional.

They usually specialize in one particular area of design, such as automobiles, clothing, furniture, home appliances, industrial equipment, movie and theater sets, and packaging. They compare similar or competitive products, taking into account and often setting fashion trends. Designers usually make sketches of several designs, which they present for final selection to an art or design director; a product development team; a play, film, or television producer; or a client. Designers in some specialties use computer-aided design (CAD) to create and better visualize a final product.

Design comprises a number of different fields. Industrial designers develop and design manufactured products. Interior designers both plan the space and furnish the interiors of private homes, public buildings, and commercial establishments, such as offices, restaurants, hotels, and theaters. Set designers design movie, television, and theater sets. Fashion designers design wearing apparel and accessories. Textile designers design fabrics for garments, upholstery, rugs, and other products, using their knowledge of textile materials and fashion trends.

Qualifications

Qualities that are crucial in all design occupations are a strong color sense, an eye for detail, a sense of balance and proportion, and sensitivity to beauty. Sketching ability is especially important for fashion designers. A good portfolio, a collection of samples of a person's best work, is often the deciding factor in landing a job. In addition, problem-solving skills and the ability to work independently are important traits. Business sense and sales ability are important for those who are freelancers or run their own businesses.

Educational requirements for entry-level positions vary. For most design positions, some formal career preparation is necessary, such as a two-year degree in design offered by professional schools.

Income and Advancement

Median weekly earnings of experienced full-time designers in all fields of design were about $585 in 1982, with the range being between $375 and $855 a week. The top 10 percent earned more than $1,120. The average base salary for an entry-level industrial designer with one to two years of experience was about $27,900. Staff designers with about six years of experience earned approximately $38,100, while seniors designers with about 10 years of experience earned about $44,500. Industrial designers with managerial or executive positions earned substantially more—up to about $75,000.

Salaries of junior interior designers in the largest interior design firms averaged $25,000; those of project and senior designers, approximately $38,000. Project managers averaged about $50,500.

Where to Get More Information

For a list of accredited schools of art and design, contact:

National Association of Schools of Art and Design, 11250 Roger Bacon Dr., Reston, VA 22090.

For career information, write to:

Industrial Designers Society of American, 1142-E Walker Rd., Great Falls, VA 22066.

American Society for Interior Designers, 608 Massachusetts Ave., NE, Washington, DC 20002.

Foundation for Interior Education Research, 60 Monroe Center, NW, Grand Rapids, MI 49503.

American Society of Furniture Designers, P.O. Box 2688, High Point, NC 27261.

Photographer and Camera Operator

Job Description

Everybody likes to look at pictures, whether they are family photographs; newspaper, magazine, or book illustrations; movies; or television programs. The job of a photographer or camera operator is to portray people, places, and events accurately or artistically. Skillful photographers also create the special feeling or mood that sells products, presents ideas, highlights news stories, or brings back memories. Photography is also an art medium. As in other art forms, self-expression and creativity are central, while technical proficiency—essential for producing special effects—provides the vehicle for conveying the artist's message.

Camera operators generally use 35- or 16-millimeter cameras or camcorders to film commercial motion pictures and documentary or industrial films. They also make films for news and film private ceremonies and special events.

Photographers use a wide variety of cameras that can accept lenses designed for close-up, medium-range, or distance photography. The cameras also offer adjustments that give the photographers creative and technical control over the picture-taking process. In addition, photographers and camera operators use an array of equipment—from film, filters, tripods, and flash attachments to specially constructed motorized vehicles and special lighting. Many photographers develop and print their own photographs. Most, however, send their film to laboratories for processing.

Photographers may specialize in such areas as commercial, portrait, or journalistic photography. Many portrait photographers are small-business owners who set and adjust equipment, develop and retouch negatives, and mount and frame pictures.

Commercial, editorial, and industrial photographers take pictures of such subjects as manufactured articles, buildings, and groups of people. Their work is used in reports, advertisements, and catalogs. Industrial photographers take photographs or videotapes for use in analyzing engineering projects, for publicity, or as records of equipment and processes.

Scientific photographers provide illustrations and documentation for scientific publications, research reports, and textbooks. Biomedical photographers may take photographs of medical procedures, such as surgery.

Some camera operators work for television stations covering news events; others are employed in the entertainment field, using motion picture cameras to film movies or electronicaly record movies, television programs, and commercials.

Most salaried photographers work in photographic portrait or commercial photography studios. Others are with newspapers, magazines, advertising agencies, and government agencies. Most camera operators are employed in television broadcasting or in motion picture studios.

Qualifications

Learning on the job is a good approach for fashion, commercial, and portrait photography. Camera operators also generally acquire their skills this way. Photography assistants may learn to mix chemicals, develop film, and print photographs. Community and junior colleges, vocational-technical institutes, and private trade and technical schools offer courses in photography, often as part of a communications or journalism program. Basic courses in photography are also available through home-study programs offered by correspondence schools. Photographers and camera operators need good eyesight, artistic ability, and manual dexterity. Knowledge of mathematics, physics, and chemistry is helpful for understanding the workings of lenses, films, light sources, and developing processes.

Income and Advancement

The median annual earnings for salaried photographers and camera operators who work full time were about $21,200 in 1992, with income ranging from $16,500 to $35,000. The top 10 percent earned more than $49,200.

For self-employed photographers, earnings are affected by the number of hours worked, their skills, their marketing ability, and general business conditions.

Where to Get More Information

Professional Photographers of America, Inc., 1090 Executive Way, Des Plaines, IL 60018.

American Society of Media Photographers, Suite 502-14, Washington Rd., Princeton Junction, NJ 08550.

Eastman Information Center, 343 State St., Rochester, NY 14650.

New York Institute of Photography (home-study programs), 211 E. 43rd St., New York, NY 10017.

Radio and Television Announcer and Newscaster

Job Description

Announcers, newscasters, and sports reporters are well-known personalities to radio and TV audiences throughout the nation. Radio announcers, also known as disk jockeys, introduce and play recorded music and present national and local news, sports events, weather, and commercials. They introduce guests and report on local activities of interest to their listeners and viewers. The may do their own research and write their own scripts, and they often ad-lib much of their commentary.

At large stations, announcers usually specialize in sports and weather, or in general news. Some are news analysts. In small stations, one announcer may perform all these functions. News anchors introduce in-depth videotaped news or live transmissions from on-the-scene reporters. Weather reporters report and forecast weather conditions using information gathered from national satellite weather services, wire services, and other local and regional weather bureaus. Sportscasters write and deliver the local and national sports news. They interview sports personalities and present live coverage of games.

News analysts, or commentators, present news stories, interpret them, and discuss how they may affect the nation or local residents.

Since many broadcasting stations are on the air 24 hours a day, announcers work unusual hours and have to be available for tight schedules and emergency coverage of special news and events.

Nearly all radio and television announcers and newscasters work on staff, but some workers are freelancers who sell their services for individual assignments to networks and stations and independent producers.

Qualifications

Formal training in broadcast journalism is valuable. Courses are available at many community and junior colleges and private broadcasting schools. Station managers pay particular attention to taped auditions that show an applicant's delivery, appearance, and style. Those hired by television stations usually start out as production secretaries, production assistants, researchers, or reporters, and are given a chance to move into announcing if they show an aptitude for "on-air" work. Beginners landing a job with small stations usually start out recording interviews and operating equipment.

Announcers must have a pleasant voice, excellent pronunciation, and, for jobs with television stations, a pleasing appearance.

Income and Advancement

Salaries vary widely. They are higher in television than in radio, higher in large markets than in small ones, and higher in commercial than in public broadcasting.

According to a survey conducted by the National Association of Broadcasters and the Broadcast Cable Financial Management Association, the median salary for experienced radio announcers is about $18,000 a year and ranges from about $13,000 in the smallest markets to $54,000 in the largest markets for on-air personalities.

Among television announcers and news anchors, the median salary is about $52,000, ranging from $26,000 in the smallest to $163,000 in the largest markets. Weathercasters' salaries range from $25,200 to $103,320. Salaries for sportscasters range from $22,000 to $142,500. A relatively few nationally known TV news and sports announcers earn income in the middle and high six-figure range.

Where to Get More Information

For a list of schools that offer programs and courses in broadcasting and general information on the broadcasting industry, contact:

Broadcasting Education Association, 1771 N St., NW, Washington, DC 20036.

For information on careers in broadcast news, contact:

Radio-Television News Directors Association, 1717 K St., NW, Washington, DC 20006.

Visual Artist

Job Description

Visual artists communicate ideas, thoughts, and feelings by creating realistic and abstract works, using a variety of methods and materials. These include oil, watercolors, acrylics, pastels, pencils, pen and ink, silkscreen, plaster, clay, and any of a number of other media, including computers.

Artists generally fall into one of two categories—"graphic artists" and "fine artists"—depending on the artists's purpose in creating the work. Graphic artists create work for commercial clients, such as corporations, retail stores, and advertising, design, or publishing firms. Fine artists often create art to satisfy their need for self-expression and may display their work in museums, art galleries, and homes.

Fine artists usually work independently, specializing in one or two forms of art. Painters generally work with two-dimensional art forms, creating works that depict realistic scenes or abstract visualizations to evoke different moods and emotions. Sculptors design three-dimensional art works, either molding and joining materials such as clay, wire, plastic, or metal, or cutting and carving forms from a block of plaster, wood, or stone. Some combine various materials such as concrete, metal, wood, plastic, and paper.

Printmakers create printed images from designs cut into wood, stone, or metal, or from computer-driven data. These designs then may be engraved, as in the case of woodblocking; etched, as in the production of etchings; or derived from computers in the form of inked prints.

Some fine artists preserve and restore damaged and faded paintings by applying solvents and cleaning agents to clean the surface, reconstructing rough or damaged areas, and applying preservatives to protect the paintings.

Fine artists may sell their works to stores, commercial art galleries, and museums, or directly to collectors. Only the most successful fine artists are able to support themselves solely through sale of their works, making it necessary for them to hold other jobs as well.

Graphic artists, whether freelancers or those employed by a company, use a variety of print and film media to create art that meets a client's needs. They are increasingly using computers to produce their work. Computers enable them to lay out and test various designs, formats, and colors before printing a final design.

Graphic artists perform different jobs depending on their area of expertise. Graphic designers may create packaging and promotional displays, the visual design of an annual report, or a distinctive logo for a product or business. They also help with the layout and design of magazines, newspapers, journals, and other publications; films; and paper products, such as greeting cards, calendars, and stationery. Many do a variety of illustrations.

Medical and scientific illustrators draw parts of the human body, animals, plants, and surgical procedures, which are used in medical textbooks and in slide and video presentations for teaching purposes.

Fashion artists draw illustrations of women's, men's, and children's clothing and accessories for newspapers, magazines, and other media.

Some illustrators draw "story boards" for TV commercials. Story boards present commercials in a series of scenes so that an advertising agency and client can evaluate the proposed commercials.

Cartoonists draw political, advertising, social, and sports cartoons. Cartoonists should have humorous, critical, or dramatic talents in addition to drawing skills.

Animators work in the motion picture and television industries, drawing the large series of pictures that, when transferred to film or tape, form the animated cartoons seen in movies and on TV.

Art directors read the material to be printed in periodicals, newspapers, and other printed media, and decide how to present the information visually in an eye-catching manner. They make decisions about which photographs or artwork are to be used and, in general, oversee production of the printed material.

About three out of five visual artists are either self-employed, offering their services to advertising agencies, publishing firms, and other businesses, or fine artists who earn income when they sell a painting or other art work.

Qualifications

In the fine arts field, formal training requirements do not exist, but some training is desirable. In the graphic arts field, demonstrated ability and appropriate training are necessary. Evidence of talent and skill should be represented in the artist's portfolio. The portfolio is a collection of handmade, computer-generated, or printed examples of the artist's best work. Employers and art directors require that a job applicant present his or her portfolio in interviews.

Aspiring artists should take high school courses in art and design. Many two-year community colleges and junior colleges have programs in commercial art, while private schools offer courses in both fine art and commercial art. For those who want to advance into higher education, college and universities offer four-year programs leading to a degree in fine arts.

Income and Advancement

Whereas starting salaries are relatively low, salaries for experienced visual artists who work full time range from about $21,400 to more than $43,500 per year. Fine artists and illustrators advance as they establish their reputations. Graphic artists may advance to assistant art director, art director, or design director. Advertising agency and publishing art directors can earn $75,000 a year and more.

Where to Get More Information

The Association of Medical Illustrators, 1819 Peachtree St., NE, Atlanta, GA 30309.

The American Institute of Graphic Arts, 1059 Third Ave., New York, NY 10021.

The Society of Publication Designers, 60 E. 42nd St., Suite 1416, New York, NY 10165.

CONSTRUCTION

Bricklayer and Stonemason

Job Description

Bricklayers and stonemasons work in trades that produce attractive, durable surfaces and structures. Bricklayers build walls, floors, partitions, fireplaces, chimneys, and other structures with brick, precast masonry panels, concrete block, and other masonry materials. Stonemasons build stone walls as well as set stone exteriors and floors. They work with two types of stone: natural cut, such as marble, granite, and limestone; and artificial stone, which is made from concrete marble chips or other masonry materials. Stonemasons usually work on large structures, such as churches, hotels, hospitals, and office buildings.

Bricklayers are assisted by hod carriers, or helpers, who bring brick and other materials, mix mortar, and set up and move scaffolding.

Stonemasons often work from a set of drawings in which each stone has been numbered for identification. When building a stone wall, masons align the stones with wedges, plumblines, and levels, and adjust them into position with a hard rubber mallet. They build the wall by alternating layers of mortar and courses of stone.

Refractory masons are bricklayers who install firebrick and refractory file in high-temperature boilers, furnaces, cupolas, ladles, and soaking pits in industrial plants. Most work in steel mills, where molten materials flow on refractory beds from furnaces to rolling machines.

Workers in these crafts are employed primarily by special trade, building, or general contractors. About one of every four bricklayers and stonemasons is self-employed; many specialize in contracting on small jobs such as patios, walks, and fireplaces.

Qualifications

Most bricklayers and stonemasons pick up their skills by observing and learning from experienced workers. Many get training in vocational schools. The best way to learn these skills, however, is through an apprenticeship program.

Apprenticeships for bricklayers and stonemasons usually are sponsored by local contractors or by local union management committees. Applicants for apprenticeships must be at least 17 years old and in good physical condition. A high school education is preferable, and courses in mathematics, mechanical drawing, and shop are helpful.

Income and Advancement

Median weekly earnings for bricklayers and stonemasons are about $408. The middle 50 percent earn between $335 and $640, while the highest 10 percent earn more than $838 a week.

Experienced workers can advance to supervisory positions or become estimators. They can open contracting businesses of their own. Some bricklayers and stonemasons are members of the International Union of Bricklayers and Allied Craftsmen.

Where to Get More Information

For details about apprenticeships, contact the nearest office of the state employment service or state apprenticeship agency.

For general information about the work, contact:

International Union of Bricklayers and Allied Craftsmen, International Masonry Institute Apprenticeship and Training, 815 15th St., NW, Washington, DC 20005.

Associated General Contractors of America, Inc., 1957 E St., NW, Washington, DC 20006.

Brick Institute of America, 11490 Commerce Park Dr., Reston, VA 22091.

National Concrete Masonry Association, 2302 Horse Pen Rd., Herndon, VA 22071.

Carpenter

Job Description

Carpenters work with many different kinds of materials besides wood, such as plastic, ceiling tile, fiberglass, and drywall. Working from blueprints or instructions from supervisors, carpenters first do the layout—measuring, marking, and arranging materials. Local building codes often dictate where certain material can be used, and carpenters have to know these requirements.

Carpenters cut, fit, and assemble materials in the construction of buildings, highways and bridges, docks, industrial plants, boats, and many other structures. They use hand and power tools, such as chisels, planes, saws, drills, and sanders. They then join the materials with nails, screws, staples, or adhesives.

Workers employed outside the construction industry do a variety of installation and maintenance work. They may replace panes of glass, ceiling tiles, and doors, as well as repair desks, cabinets, and other furniture. Depending on the employer, carpenters may install partitions, doors, and windows; change locks; and repair broken furniture.

Qualifications

Carpenters learn their trade through on-the-job training and through formal training programs. Some pick up skills informally by working under the supervision of experienced workers. Many acquire skills through vocational education. Others participate in employer training programs or apprenticeships.

On the job, apprentices learn elementary structural design and become familiar with such carpentry jobs as layout, form building, rough framing, and outside and inside finishing. They also learn to use tools, machines, equipment, and materials of the trade. Classroom training includes instruction in blueprint reading and freehand sketching, basic mathematics, and different carpentry techniques. Both in the classroom and on the job, they learn the relationship between carpentry and the other building trades.

A high school education is desirable, including courses in carpentry, shop, mechanical drawing, and general mathematics. Manual dexterity, eye-hand coordination, and a good sense of balance are important. The ability to solve arithmetic problems quickly and accurately also is helpful.

Income and Advancement

Median weekly earnings of carpenters who were not self-employed were $425 in 1992. The middle 50 percent earned between $320 and $585 per week, with the top 10 percent earning more than $770 per week.

Carpenters may advance to carpentry supervisors in general construction. They usually have greater opportunities than most other construction workers to become general construction supervisor because they are exposed to the entire construction process. Some carpenters become independent contractors. A large proportion of carpenters are members of the United Brotherhood of Carpenters and Joiners of America.

Where to Get More Information

Associated Builders and Contractors, 729 15th St., NW, Washington, DC 20005.

Home Builders Institute, Educational Arm of the National Association of Home Builders, 1090 Vermont Ave., NW, Washington, DC 20005.

Associated General Contractors of America, 1957 E St., NW, Washington, DC 20006.

United Brotherhood of Carpenters and Joiners of America, 101 Constitution Ave., NW, Washington, DC 20001.

Concrete Mason

Job Description

Concrete is all around us, in our sidewalks, our buildings, and our highways and roads. A mixture of portland cement, sand, gravel, and water, concrete is used for many types of construction projects. These range from small jobs such as patios and floors, to huge dams or miles of highways.

Concrete masons are the workers who place and finish the concrete for these projects. In preparing a site for placing concrete, masons set forms for holding the concrete for the desired pitch and depth and properly align them. They then direct the casting of the concrete and supervise laborers who use shovels or special tools to spread the concrete. Masons then guide a straightedge back and forth across the top of the forms to "screed," or level, the freshly placed concrete.

On concrete surfaces that will remain exposed after forms are stripped, such as columns, ceilings, and wall panels, concrete masons cut away high spots and loose concrete with hammer and chisel, fill any large indentations with a portland cement paste, and smooth the surface with a rubbing carborundum stone. Finally, they coat the exposed area with a rich portland cement mixture, using either a special tool or a coarse cloth to rub the concrete to a uniform finish.

Most concrete masons work for concrete contractors or for general contractors on such projects as highways, bridges, shopping malls, or large building such as factories, schools, and hospitals. A small number are employed by firms that manufacture concrete products. A small percentage of masons is self-employed; most specialize in small jobs, such as driveways, sidewalks, and patios.

Qualifications

Concrete masons learn their trades either through on-the-job training as helpers or through two- or three-year apprenticeship programs. Many masons first gain experience as construction laborers. On-the-job training programs consist of informal instruction from experienced workers in which helpers learn to use the tools, equipment, machines, and materials of the trade. As they progress, assignments become more complex, and trainees usually can do finishing work within a short time.

Two- and three-year apprenticeship programs, usually jointly sponsored by local unions and contractors, provide on-the-job training in addition to a recommended minimum of 144 hours of classroom instruction each year. A written test and a physical exam may be required. In the classroom, apprentices learn applied mathematics, plan reading, and safety. Apprentices generally receive special instruction in layout work and cost estimating.

When hiring helpers and apprentices, employers prefer high school graduates who are in good physical condition and licensed to drive. The ability to get along with others is also important because concrete masons frequently work in teams. High school courses in shop mathematics and blueprint reading or mechanical drawing provide a helpful background. As the population and economy grows, more masons will be needed to build highways, bridges, industrial plants, office building, hotels, shopping centers, schools, hospitals, and other structures. In addition, the increasing use of concrete as a building material, particularly in nonresidential construction, will add to the demand. Masons will also be needed to repair and renovate existing highways, bridges, and other structures.

Income and Advancement

According to limited information available, average hourly earnings, including benefits, for concrete masons who belonged to a union and worked full time ranged between $15 and $37 in 1992. Experienced concrete masons may become supervisors or contract estimators. Some open concrete contracting businesses.

Where to Get More Information

For information about apprenticeships and work opportunities, contact local concrete contractors, locals of unions previously mentioned, or the nearest office of the state employment service or apprenticeship agency.

For general information, contact:

Associated General Contractors of America, Inc., 1957 E St., NW, Washington, DC 20006.

International Union of Bricklayers and Allied Craftsmen, 815 15th St., NW, Washington, DC 20005.

Portland Cement Association, 5420 Old Orchard Rd., Skokie, IL 60077.

National Terrazzo and Mosaic Association, 3166 Des Plaines Ave., Des Plaines, IL 60018.

Construction and Building Inspector

Job Description

Buildings, highways, streets, sewer and water systems, dams, bridges, and tunnels are required to comply with building codes, ordinances, zoning regulations, and contract specifications. The job of construction and building inspectors is to examine the construction, alteration, or repair of these and other structures to ensure that all laws and regulations are observed. They make the initial inspections during the first phase of construction, and they make follow-up inspections throughout the construction period, to monitor continuing compliance.

Building inspectors inspect the structural quality and general safety of buildings. Some may specialize, for example, in structural steel or concrete buildings. Electrical inspectors inspect the installation of electrical systems and equipment to ensure that they function properly and comply with electrical codes and standards. Elevator inspectors examine lifting and conveying devices, such as elevators, escalators, moving sidewalks, personnel lifts and hoists, inclined railways, ski lifts, and amusement rides. Mechanical inspectors inspect the installation of the mechanical components of commercial kitchen appliances, heat and air-conditioning equipment, gasoline and butane tanks, and gas and oil piping. Public works inspectors ensure that federal, state, and local government construction of water and sewer systems, highways, streets, bridges, and dams conforms to detailed contract specifications. Home inspectors check newly built homes to ascertain adherence to regulatory requirements. Some home inspectors are hired by prospective home buyers to inspect and report on the condition of the home's major systems. Home inspectors typically are hired either immediately prior to a purchase offer or as a contingency to a sales contract.

When something is discovered that does not comply with the appropriate codes, ordinances, contract specifications, or approved plans, inspectors notify the contractor or supervisor. If the deficiency is not corrected within a reasonable specified time, government inspectors have authority to issue a "stop-work" order.

Nearly three-fifths of construction and building inspectors work for local municipal and county governments. One-fifth of inspectors are employed at the federal and state levels. Most of the remaining inspectors work for firms in the engineering and architectural services, construction, and business services industries.

Qualifications

Construction and building inspectors need several years of experience as a construction contractor, supervisor, or craft worker before becoming inspectors. Most employers also require applicants to have a high school diploma. High school courses in drafting, algebra, geometry, and English are also useful. Employers also prefer people who have graduated from an apprenticeship program; have studied engineering or architecture for at least two years; or have a degree from a community or junior college, with courses in construction technology, blueprint reading, and mathematics. Many construction and building inspectors have recent experience as carpenters, electricians, plumbers, or pipefitters. Many employers provide formal training programs to broaden inspectors' knowledge.

Income and Advancement

The median annual salary of construction and building inspectors is about $31,200 annually, with salaries ranging from $25,000 to $51,000 and above. Certification increases chances for higher-paying, more responsible positions. Some states and cities require certification for employment. Inspectors with substantial experience and education can attain certification by taking correspondence courses or by attending seminars sponsored by the organizations listed in the following section.

Where to Get More Information

International Conference of Building Officials, 5360 S. Workman Mill Rd., Whittier, CA 90601.

Building Officials and Code Administrators International, Inc., 4051 West Flossmoor Rd., Country Club Hills, IL 60478.

Electrician

Job Description

Energy for our light, power, climate control, security, communications, and other essential systems depends upon an uninterrupted flow of electricity. To ensure that electricity is always available and operating at required capacity, electricians install and maintain the electronic controls for machines in business, industry, and the home.

Electricians work with blueprints when they install electrical systems in factories, office buildings, homes, and other structures. These blueprints indicate the location of circuits, outlets, load centers, panel boards, and other equipment. Electricians must follow the National Electric Code and comply with state and local building codes when they install these systems.

In addition to wiring a building's electrical system, electricians may install coaxial or fiber-optic cable for computers and other telecommunications equipment. A growing number of electricians install telephone and computer wiring and equipment. They may also connect motors to electrical power and install electronic controls for industrial equipment.

Qualifications

The best way to learn the electrical trade is by completing a four- or five-year apprenticeship program. This gives trainees a thorough knowledge of all aspects of the trade and generally improves their ability to find a job. Although more electricians are trained through apprenticeship than workers in other construction jobs, some still learn their skills informally on the job.

Apprenticeship programs are usually sponsored by joint training committees made up of local unions of the International Brotherhood of Electrical Workers and local chapters of the National Electrical Contractors Association. Training may also be provided by company management committees.

Those who do not enter a formal apprenticeship program can begin to learn the trade informally by working as helpers for experienced electricians.

High school courses in mathematics, electricity, electronics, mechanical drawing, science, and shop provide a good background. Most apprenticeship sponsors require applicants to be at least 18 years old and have a high school diploma or its equivalent.

Most localities require electricians to be licensed. Although licensing requirements vary from area to area, electricians generally must pass an examination that tests their knowledge of electrical theory, the National Electrical Code, and local electric and building codes.

Income and Advancement

Median weekly earnings for full-time electricians who were not self-employed were $550 in 1992. The middle 50 percent earned between $412 and $717 weekly, with the highest 10 percent earning more than $887.

Experienced electricians can become supervisors and then superintendents. Those with sufficient capital and management skills may start their own contracting business.

Where to Get More Information

For details about apprenticeships, contact the nearest office of the state employment service or state apprenticeship agency.

For general information about the work of electricians, contact:

Independent Electrical Contractors, Inc., P.O. Box 10379, Alexandria, VA 22310.

National Electrical Contractors Association (NECA), 3 Bethesda Metro Center #1100, Bethesda, MD 20814.

International Brotherhood of Electrical Workers (IBEW), 1125 15th St., NW, Washington, DC 20005.

Associated Builders and Contractors, 1300 N. 17th St., Rosslyn, VA 22209.

Plumber and Pipefitter

Job Description

We are all familiar with the plumber who comes to the house to unclog a drain or install an appliance. Plumbers and pipefitters, however, do much more than routine household repairs. They install, maintain, and repair many different types of pipe systems. For example, they work on systems that move water to municipal water treatment plants and then to residential, commercial, and public buildings. Others maintain systems that dispose of waste. Some work on pipes that bring in gas for stoves and furnaces. Still others install air-conditioning systems and work on pipes that are used in manufacturing plants to move material through the production process.

Although plumbing and pipefitting sometimes are considered a single trade, workers generally specialize in one or the other. Plumbers install and repair the water, waste disposal, drainage, and gas systems of homes and commercial and industrial buildings. They also install plumbing fixtures: bathtubs, showers, sinks, and toilets, and appliances, such as dishwashers and water heaters. Pipefitters install and repair both high- and low-pressure pipe systems that are used in manufacturing, in the generation of electricity, and in heating and cooling buildings.

Plumbers and pipefitters use many different materials and construction techniques, depending on the type of project. Residential water systems, for example, use copper, plastic, and steel pipe that can be handled and installed by one or two workers. Municipal sewerage systems, on the other hand, are made of large cast-iron pipes, and installation normally requires crews of pipefitters.

Construction plumbers work from blueprints or drawings that show the planned location of pipes, plumbing fixtures, and appliances. Sometimes they have to cut holes in walls, ceiling, and floors. For some systems, they may have to hang steel supports from ceiling joists to hold the pipe in place. After the piping is in place, plumbers install the fixtures and appliances and connect the sections and fittings with adhesives.

After the piping is in place, plumbers install the fixtures and appliances and connect the system to the outside water or sewer lines. Using pressure gauges, they check the system to ensure that the plumbing works properly.

About two-thirds of plumbers and pipefitters work for mechanical and plumbing contractors engaged in new construction, repair, modernization, or maintenance work. Others do maintenance work for a variety of industrial, commercial, and government employers. One of every six plumbers and pipefitters is self-employed.

Qualifications

Almost all plumbers undergo some type of apprenticeship training. Apprenticeships, both union and nonunion, consist of four to five years of on-the-job training in addition to at least 144 hours annually of related classroom instruction. Subjects include drafting and blueprint reading, mathematics, applied physics and chemistry, safety, and local plumbing codes and regulations. On-the-job apprentices first learn such basic skills as identifying grades and types of pipe, the use of tools, and the safe unloading of materials.

Applicants for union or nonunion apprenticeship committees may require applicants to have a high school diploma or its equivalent. High school or vocational school courses in shop, plumbing, general mathematics, drafting, blueprint reading, and physics also are good preparation.

Income and Advancement

Hourly wage rates for maintenance pipefitters in metropolitan areas range from about $16.15 to $19.68.

Some plumbers and pipefitters may become supervisors for mechanical and plumbing contractors. Others go into business for themselves.

Many plumbers and pipefitters are members of the United Association of Journeymen and Apprentices of the Plumbing and Pipe Fitting Industry of the United States and Canada.

Where to Get More Information

For information about apprenticeships or work opportunities in plumbing and pipefitting, contact local plumbing, heating, and air-conditioning contractors, or the local office of your state employment service. Other sources of information are the following:

Home Builders Institute, 1090 Vermont Ave., NW, Washington, DC 20005.

National Association of Plumbing-Heating-Cooling Contractors, P.O. Box 6808, Falls Church, VA 22046.

Associated Builders and Contractors, 729 15th St., NW, Washington, DC 20005.

Mechanical Contractors Association of America, 1385 Picard Dr., Rockville, MD 20850.

Sheet Metal Worker

Job Description

Sheet metal workers make, install, and maintain air-conditioning, heating, ventilation, and pollution control duct systems, roofs, siding, rain gutters, restaurant equipment, skylights, outdoor signs, and many other building parts and products made from metal sheets. They may also work with fiberglass and plastic materials.

Sheet metal is usually fabricated at a shop away from the construction site. Workers measure, cut, bend, shape, and fasten pieces of metal to make duct work, counter tops, and other custom products. In many shops, they use computerized metalworking equipment.

Before assembling the individual pieces, sheet metal workers check each part for accuracy and, if necessary, finish it by using hand, rotary, or squaring shears and hacksaws. They fasten the seams and joints together with welds, bolts, cement, rivets, solder, specially formed sheet metal clips, or other connecting devices. The parts are then taken to the construction site where they are further assembled and installed.

Qualifications

Sheet metal contractors consider apprenticeship the best way to learn this trade. The program consists of four or five years of on-the-job training and a minimum of 144 hours per year of classroom instruction. Apprenticeship programs provide comprehensive instruction in both sheet metal fabrication and installation. They are administered by local joint committees composed of the Sheet Metal Workers' International Association and local chapters of the Sheet Metal and Air-Conditioning Contractors National Association, or by local chapters of the Associated Builders and Contractors.

Apprentices learn the basics of pattern layout and how to cut, bend, fabricate, and install sheet metal. In the classroom, they learn drafting; plan and specification reading; trigonometry and geometry, applicable to layout work; the use of computerized equipment; welding; and the principles of heating, air-conditioning, and ventilating systems.

Applicants for jobs as apprentices should be in good physical condition and have mechanical and mathematical aptitude, good eye-hand coordination, spatial and form perception, and manual dexterity. A high school education or its equivalent is usually required. Courses in algebra, trigonometry, geometry, mechanical, and shop provide a helpful background for learning the trade.

Income and Advancement

Pay rates vary greatly. According to available statistics, average hourly earnings, including benefits, for union sheet metal workers are about $27.62, ranging from a low of $18.06 to $42.47, depending upon the geographical location and the size of the company. Sheet metal workers may advance to supervisory jobs. Some take additional training in welding and do more specialized work. Others go into the contracting business for themselves.

A large proportion of sheet metal workers are members of the Sheet Metal Workers' International Association.

Where to Get More Information

The Sheet Metal National Training Fund, 601 N. Fairfax St., Alexandria, VA 22314.

Associated Builders and Contractors, 1300 N. 17th St., NW, Rosslyn, VA 22209.

The Sheetmetal and Air Conditioning Contractors Association, 4201 Lafayette Center Dr., Chantilly, VA 22021.

The Sheet Metal Workers International Association, 1750 New York Ave., NW, Washington, DC 20006.

Structural and Reinforcing Ironworker

Job Description

Materials made from iron, steel, aluminum, and bronze are used extensively in the construction of highways, bridges, large buildings, power transmission towers, and other structures. These structures have frames made of steel columns, beams, and girders. Reinforced concrete used in many of the nations's structures use steel bars or wire fabric for additional strength. Metal stairways, catwalks, floor gratings, ladders, and window frames, as well as lampposts, railings, fences, and decorative ironwork are used to make these structures more functional and attractive. Structural and reinforcing ironworkers fabricate, assemble, and install these products.

Before construction can begin, ironworkers must erect the steel frames and assemble the cranes and derricks that move structural steel, reinforcing bars, buckets of concrete, lumber, and others materials and equipment around the construction site. After this equipment arrives at the site, it is lifted into position by a mobile crane. Ironworkers then connect the sections and set up the cables that do the hoisting.

Ironworkers begin to connect steel columns, beams, and girders according to blueprints and instructions from supervisors and superintendents. Structural steel, reinforcing rods, and ornamental iron generally are delivered to the construction site ready for erection, cut to the proper size with holes drilled for bolts and numbered for assembly. This work is done by ironworkers in fabricating shops located away from the construction site. Ornamental ironwork and related pieces are installed after the exterior of the building has been completed.

Qualifications

Most employers recommend apprenticeship as the best way to learn this trade. Programs are usually administered by joint union-management committees. In the classroom, apprentices study blueprint reading, mathematics for layout work, the basics of structural erecting, rigging, reinforcing, welding and burning, ornamental erection, and assembling.

Some ironworkers learn informally on the job. With experience, they perform more difficult tasks such as cutting and fitting different parts. Ironworkers generally must be at least 18 years old. A high school diploma may be preferred and may be required by some local apprenticeship committees. Because materials used in ironworking are heavy and bulky, ironworkers must be in good physical condition.

Income and Advancement

Prevailing union wage rates, including benefits, averaged about $27 an hour in 1992, ranging from a low of about $18 to a high of between $38-$49, depending on the geographical location and the size of the company. Some experienced workers become supervisors. Others may go into the contracting business for themselves. Many workers in this trade are members of the International Association of Bridge, Structural and Ornamental Ironworkers.

Where to Get More Information

Associated General Contractors of America, Inc., 1300 N. 17th St., Rosslyn, VA 22209.

International Association of Bridge, Structural and Ornamental Iron Workers, 1750 New York Ave., NW, Washington, DC 20006.

National Association of Reinforcing Steel Contractors, P.O. Box 280, Fairfax, VA 22030.

Surveyor

Job Description

Surveying is the science and art of mapping or determining the area and configuration of portions of the surface of the earth. Surveyors fall into three working categories.

Land surveyors establish official land, water, and air space boundaries. They write descriptions of land for leases, deeds, and other legal documents; define air space for airports; and measure construction and mineral sites.

Survey technicians operate surveying instruments and collect information.

Mapping scientists and other surveyors collect geographic information and prepare maps and charts.

Land surveyors and technicians measure distances, directions, and angles between points, and determine the precise location of all important features of the area. They search for evidence of previous boundaries, record the results of the survey, verify the accuracy of data, and prepare maps and reports.

A typical survey party is made up of a party chief and several survey technicians, who operate such instruments as the theodolite (used to measure horizontal and vertical angles) and electron distance-measuring equipment. Survey technicians make sketches and enter the data observed from these instruments and computers.

For larger surveying projects, they use the Global Positioning System (GPS), a system that precisely locates points on the earth by using radio signals transmitted by satellites. Mapping scientists, like land surveyors, map and chart the earth's surface. They usually work from offices and may seldom or never visit the sites they are mapping. Mapping scientists include workers in other occupations. For instance, cartographers prepare maps using information provided by geodetic surveys. Photogrammetrists prepare maps and drawings by measuring and interpreting aerial photographs and make detailed maps of areas that are inaccessible or difficult to survey by other means. Map editors develop and verify map contents from aerial photographs and other reference sources.

Geophysical prospecting surveyors mark sites for exploration for oil and gas. Marine surveyors survey harbors, rivers, and other bodies of water to determine shorelines, bottom topography, and water depth.

Most surveyors in state and local governments work for departments of highways and urban planning agencies.

Qualifications

Junior and community colleges, technical institutes, and vocational schools offer one-, two-, and three-year programs in both surveying and surveying technology. High school graduates interested in surveying should take courses in algebra, geometry, trigonometry, drafting, and mechanical drawing.

High school graduates with no formal training in surveying usually start as helpers. Beginners with postsecondary school training in surveying can generally start as technicians.

Income and Advancement

According to limited data, the median annual earnings for surveyors and technicians are about $25,800. Salaries range from $17,900 to more than $40,000 a year, depending on the level of education completed and years of experience. Workers may advance to senior survey technician, then to party chief and, finally, to licensed surveyor.

Technicians who want to pursue additional education and earn a bachelor's degree in surveying can improve their chances of advancement to higher supervisory positions in the field.

Where to Get More Information

American Congress on Surveying and Mapping, 5410 Grosvenor Lane, Bethesda, MD 20814.

American Society for Photogrammetry and Remote Sensing, 5410 Grosvenor Lane, Bethesda, MD 20814.

FORESTRY AND FISHING

Fisher, Hunter, and Trapper

Job Description

Fishers, hunters, and trappers perform a wide range of occupational functions, reflecting the variety of marine and animal life and their environmental conditions. They gather marine and animal life for human consumption and for animal feed, bait, and other industrial uses; and they manage animal life for research and control purposes.

Harvesting sea life hundreds of miles from shore with large boats capable of hauling tens of thousands of pounds of fish requires a crew of up to 30 fishers: a captain, a first mate and sometimes a second mate, boatswains, and other deckhands.

The captain plans and oversees the fishing operation, ensuring that the fishing vessel is in suitable condition; oversees the purchase of fuel, netting, cables, gear, and other equipment; and hires qualified crew members and assigns their duties. Upon returning to port, the captain arranges for the sale of the catch directly to buyers or through a fish auction and ensures that each crew member receives the prearranged portion of the adjusted net proceeds from the sale of the catch.

The mate, the captain's assistant, assumes control of the vessel when the captain is off duty. Boatswains—highly experienced deck hands with supervisory responsibilities—and other deckhands carry out the sailing and fishing operations.

Vessels may also be used for diving operations. Depending on the water's depth, fishers, wearing a regulation diving suit with an air line or a scuba outfit and equipment, use spears to catch fish and nets and other equipment to gather shellfish, coral, and sponges. They use a variety of hand-operated equipment, such as nets, tongs, rakes, hoes, hooks, and shovels, to gather fin fish and shellfish, and to catch water animals, such as frogs, turtles, and other marine life.

While most are involved with commercial fishing, some captains and deckhands are primarily involved with recreational and sport fishing.

Hunters track, stalk, and kill their quarry. They usually operate alone or as members of a small hunting party. They use guns and bows and arrows to hunt certain preditory and game animals in accordance with official governmental guidelines established for animal control programs. A few hunters are involved in photographing or collecting animals for museums.

Trappers catch animals or birds using baited, scented, or camouflaged traps, snares, cages, or nets. Many hunters and trappers skin animals and prepare and sell the pelts and skins. Trappers also may be involved with animal damage control, wildlife management, disease control, and research activities.

Six of every 10 fishers, hunters, and trappers are self-employed. Many work part-time, particularly in the summer when demand for these workers peaks.

Captains, mates, and deckhands on fishing vessels account for the majority of the jobs. Trappers and, to a lesser extent, hunters account for the remaining jobs. Significant numbers of fishers are involved in sports fishing activities, whereas others work for museums, primarily in aquariums, oceanariums, and marine museums. Small numbers are employed in many other industries.

Qualifications

Fishers generally acquire their skills on the job. No formal academic requirements exist. However, young persons can expedite their entrance into these occupations by enrolling in two-year vocational and technical programs offered by secondary schools. The University of Rhode Island offers a degree program in fishery technology that includes courses in seamanship, vessel operations, marine safety, navigation, and vessel repair and maintenance, and provides by hands-on experience.

Captains and mates on larger fishing vessels must be licensed, as must be captains of sport fishing boats used for charter. Crew members involved in fish processing on fishing vessels of at least 100 tons may need a merchant mariner's document. These documents and licenses are issued by the U.S. Coast Guard.

Most fishers start as deckhands. Those whose experience and interests are in ship engineering, maintenance, and repair can eventually become licensed chief engineers on large commercial vessels.

Hunters and trappers generally acquire their knowledge of wildlife and hunting and trapping equipment and supplies through experience. There is no formal training for hunters. Hunters and trappers must be in good health and possess physical strength and stamina.

Income and Advancement

Earnings of fishers, hunters, and trappers generally are highest in the summer and fall, when demand for their services peaks. Many full-time and most part-time workers supplement their income by working in other activities during the off-season. For example, fishers may work in seafood processing plants or in establishments selling fishing and marine equipment. Hunters may work as self-employed guides (for an outfitter, for instance) or in stores selling guns or hunting and related equipment. Trappers may work in stores that sell trapping equipment.

Earnings of fishers vary widely depending upon the specific occupational function, the size of the ship, and the amount and value of the catch. The costs of the fishing operation—operating the ship, repair and maintenance, and supplies—are deducted from the sale of the catch. The net proceeds are distributed among the crew members in accordance with a prearranged percentage. Generally, the ship's owner, usually its captain, receives half of the net proceeds, which covers any profit as well as the depreciation, maintenance, and replacement costs of the ship.

Where to Get More Information

For general information about fishing occupations, contact:

National Oceanic and Atmospheric Administration, Office of Public Affairs, 1335 East-West Highway, Silver Spring, MD 20910.

For information on licensing of captains and mates contact:

U.S. Coast Guard, 2100 Second St., SW, Washington, DC 20593.

Information on licensing of hunting guides is available from the Department of Fish and Game in your state.

Timber Cutter and Logging Worker

Job Description

To provide the raw material for countless consumer and industrial products, thousands of acres of the nation's forests are harvested for timber. The process of timber cutting and logging is carried out by a variety of workers.

Fallers cut down trees with chain saws or mechanical felling equipment.

Buckers trim off the tops of branches and buck (cut) the resulting logs into specified lengths. They usually use gas-powered chain saws.

Choker setters fasten chokers (steel chains) around logs to be skidded (dragged) by tractors or forwarded by a cable system consisting of one or more towers interconnected by cables and fixed to the ground by guy wires and tree stumps. The logs are attached to the cables, then forwarded from the felling site to the landing.

Riggers set up and dismantle the cables and guy wires of the cable yarding system.

Logging tractor operators drive crawler or wheeled tractors to skid logs from the felling site to the landing.

Some operate harvesters—tractors outfitted with specialized equipment that can cut and delimb trees. Others haul the logs to the landing and load them onto trucks.

Log handling equipment operators operate tracked or wheeled equipment to load or unload logs and pulpwood onto or off trucks or gondola railroad cars.

Log graders and scalers inspect logs for defects, measure logs to determine their volume, and estimate the marketable content or value of logs or pulpwood.

Other timber cutting and logging workers perform a variety of duties. Cruisers hike through forests to assess logging conditions and estimate the volume of marketable timber. Brush clearing laborers clear areas of brush and other growth. Tree trimmers prune treetops and branches. Pickers select and place logs onto skidders and log blocks onto conveyors to be sent to other machines for further processing. Others use sledge hammers, mallets, wedges, and froes (cleaving tools) to split logs to form posts, pickets, shakes, and other objects.

Although timber cutting and logging equipment is mechanized, many logging jobs are still labor-intensive. A skillful, experienced logger is expected to handle a variety of logging operations.

Most salaried timber cutting and logging workers are employed in the logging camps and logging contractors industry. Others work in the sawmills and planing mills and forest services industries. Although logging operations are found in most states, Oregon and Washington account for about one out of every four logging workers. Self-employed logging contractors account for three out of every 10 logging workers—a much higher proportion of self-employment than for most occupations.

Qualifications

Most timber cutting and logging workers develop their skills through on-the-job training. They must familiarize themselves with the operations of logging machinery and equipment. Instruction comes primarily from experienced workers. Larger logging companies and trade associations, however, may offer special programs, particularly for workers training to operate large, expensive machinery and equipment. Safety training is a vital part of instruction for all logging workers.

Experience in other occupations can lead to entry into various logging occupations. For example, woodworkers, such as carpenters and sawyers, can become buckers. Equipment operators, such as truck drivers and bulldozer and crane operators, can assume skidding and yarding functions. Some loggers have worked in sawmills or on family farms with extensive wooded areas.

Little formal education is required. However, many secondary schools, including vocational and technical schools, and a few community colleges offer courses in general forestry and forest harvesting. Courses in basic mathematics are recommended.

Timber cutters and logging workers must have good health, physical strength and stamina, and the desire and ability to work outdoors every day. Mechanical aptitude is necessary for operators of machinery and equipment. Initiative and managerial and business skills are necessary for success as a self-employed logging contractor.

Income and Advancement

Income for logging workers varies considerably, depending on the size of the company, geographic location, and the occupation, experience, and skill of the worker. The annual earnings of full-time logging workers range between $16,000 and $21,216, with some earning more than $29,000. Earnings of more skilled workers, such as fallers and yarder operators, are substantially higher than those of less skilled workers, such as laborers and choker setters. Earnings of workers in the largest establishments are much higher than those in the smallest establishments. Workers in Alaska and the Northwest earn substantially more than those in the south. Many logging workers in the Northwest, where the larger establishments are concentrated, are members of either one of two unions: the International Woodworkers of America or the Eastern Council of Industrial Workers.

Timber cutting and logging workers generally advance from occupations involving primarily manual labor to those involving the operation of expensive, sometimes complicated machinery and equipment. Many workers go into business for themselves as logging contractors and have the opportunity to grow and prosper in the industry.

Where to Get More Information

Northeastern Loggers Association, P.O. Box 69, Old Forge, NY 13420.

Timber Producers Association of Michigan and Wisconsin, P.O. Box 39, Tomahawk, WI 54487.

American Forest and Paper Association, 1250 Connecticut Ave., NW, Washington, DC 20036.

For further information, contact the school of forestry at your state land-grant college or university. Addresses are available in public libraries.

HEALTH SERVICES AND MEDICAL TECHNOLOGY

● ●

Clinical Laboratory and Medical Technician

Job Description

In the detection, diagnosis, and treatment of disease, laboratory testing plays a critical role. Clinical and medical laboratory technologists
perform many of these tests.

Medical laboratory personnel examine and analyze body fluids,
tissues, and cells, looking for bacteria, parasites, or other micro-
organisms, and they test for drug levels in the blood to show how a
patient is responding to treatment. They also prepare specimens for
examination, count cells, and look for abnormal cells. Clinical and
medical laboratory technicians draw blood; help prepare specimens
for chemical, hematological, microscopic, and bacterial tests; operate
automatic analyzers; perform manual tests, following detailed
instructions; and generally assist physicians, medical technologists, or
laboratory managers.

Hours and other working conditions vary according to the size
of the facility. In large hospitals or in commercial laboratories that

operate continuously, personnel usually work the day, evening, or night shift and may work weekends and holidays. Laboratories in small facilities are likely to work on rotating shifts rather than on regular shifts.

Qualifications

Medical laboratory technicians acquire their training in community and junior colleges, hospitals, or vocational and technical schools. A few acquire their training on the job. Many programs last two years and lead to an associate degree. Others are shorter and lead to a certificate in medical laboratory technology.

Clinical laboratory personnel need analytical judgment and the ability to work under pressure. Close attention to detail is essential because small differences or changes in test substances or numerical readouts can be critical for patient care. Manual dexterity and normal color vision are highly desirable.

Income and Advancement

Clinical and medical technicians employed full time average between $19,131 and $32,864 a year, with the top 10 percent earning more than $39,000. Extra pay is usually provided for overtime and for work on weekends and holidays. Further education can lead to more responsibilities and additional monetary reward.

Where to Get More Information

American Medical Technologists, 710 Higgins Rd., Park Ridge, IL 60068.

National Certification Agency for Medical Laboratory Personnel, 7910 Woodmont Ave., Bethesda, MD 20814.

International Society for Clinical Laboratory Technology, 818 Olive St., St. Louis, MO 63101

Dental Hygienist

Job Description

When you visit your dentist, you will probably meet a dental hygienist first. They perform a wide variety of services. Dental hygienists provide preventive dental care and teach patients how to practice good oral hygiene. They examine the patient's teeth and mouth, recording the presence of diseases or abnormalities. They remove plaque, expose and develop X-rays, place temporary fillings and periodontal dressings, remove sutures, and polish amalgam fillings. In some states, hygienists administer local anesthetics and place and carve filling materials.

Dental hygienists also help patients develop and maintain good oral health. They teach patients how to select toothbrushes, and they show them how to floss their teeth. They use a variety of instruments in the course of their work, such as instruments to clean teeth, X-ray machines to take dental pictures, syringes with needles to administer local anesthetics, and models of teeth to explain oral hygiene.

Flexible working hours are common. Full-time, part-time, evening, and weekend work is widely available. Dentists frequently hire hygienists to work only two or three days a week, so many hold jobs in more than one dental office. About half of all dental hygienists usually work part-time—less than 35 hours a week. Most hygienists work in private dental offices. Others work in public health agencies, school systems, hospitals, and clinics.

Qualifications

Dental hygienists must be licensed by the state in which they practice. To qualify for a license, a candidate must graduate from an accredited dental hygiene school and pass both a written and a clinical examination.

Completion of an associate degree program is sufficient for practice in a private dental office. Requirements, however, vary depending on the state in which the hygienist practices and the facility in which he or she is employed. Schools offer laboratory, clinical, and classroom instructions in such subjects as anatomy, physiology, chemistry, microbiology, pharmacology, nutrition, radiography, histology (the study of tissue structure), periodontology (the study of gum diseases), dental materials, and dental hygiene.

Dental hygienists should be able to work well with others, particularly patients who may be under stress. Personal cleanliness and good health are important qualities. They must have manual dexterity because they use dental instruments. Recommended high school courses are biology, health, chemistry, psychology, speech, and mathematics.

Income and Advancement

Earnings of dental hygienists are affected by geographic location, employment setting, and education and experience. Those who work in private dental offices may be paid on an hourly, daily, or weekly basis.

According to the American Dental Association, dental hygienists who worked 32 hours a week or more averaged $609 a week in 1991; the average hourly earnings for all dental hygienists was $18.50.

Where to Get More Information

Division of Professional Development, American Dental Hygienist Association, 444 N. Michigan Ave., Chicago, IL 60611.

SELECT, American Dental Association/American Association of Dental Schools, 211 E. Chicago Ave., Chicago, IL 60611.

Dental Laboratory Technician

Job Description

Dental laboratory technicians, like pharmacists, fill prescriptions ordered by dentists. Working from specifications, dental laboratories make crowns, bridges, dentures, and other dental prosthetics. The specifications are usually accompanied by an impression or a mold of the patient's mouth or teeth. Dental laboratory technicians then create a model of the patient's mouth by pouring plaster into the impression and allowing it to set. They place the model on an apparatus that mimics the bite and movement of the patient's jaw. This serves as a basis for the prosthetic device.

Working from the dentist's specifications, technicians use small hand instruments to build and shape a wax tooth or teeth. This wax model is used to cast the metal framework for the device. Once the wax tooth has been formed, dental technicians pour the cast and make the metal. They prepare the surface in the base and apply porcelain in layers to arrive at the precise shape and color of a tooth. The tooth is then placed in a porcelain furnace, and the porcelain is baked onto the metal framework. The final product is an exact replica of the tooth or teeth lost.

Most dental technicians work in small commercial dental laboratories with fewer than five employees. Some laboratories, however, are larger and can employ more than 50 technicians. Many dental laboratory technicians work in dentists' offices. Others work in hospitals that provide dental services.

Qualifications

Most dental laboratory technicians learn their craft on the job. Becoming a fully trained technician requires an average of three to four years, depending upon the individual's aptitude and ambition. Training in dental technology is also available through community and junior colleges and vocational or technical institutes. Programs provide classroom instruction in dental materials science, oral anatomy, fabrication procedures, ethics, and related subjects. In addition, each student is given supervised practical experience in the school of an associated dental laboratory.

To become fully qualified, graduates need to gain additional hands-on experience. Many employers will train someone without any classroom experience.

A high degree of manual dexterity, good vision, and the ability to recognize very fine color shadings and variations in shape are necessary. Useful high school courses are art, metal and wood shop, drafting, and sciences. Courses in management and business may help those wishing to operate their own businesses.

Earnings and Advancement

Wages range from about $6 an hour for beginners to about $15 an hour for experienced technicians. In larger dental laboratories, technicians may become supervisors or managers, with subsequent increases in earnings. Experienced technicians may teach or take jobs with dental suppliers in such areas as product development, marketing, or sales. For most technicians, opening one's own laboratory is the way toward advancement and higher earnings in this field. Approximately one technician in five is self-employed.

Where to Get More Information

For information about training and a list of approved schools, contact:

Commission on Dental Accreditation, American Dental Association, 211 E. Chicago Ave., Chicago, IL 60611.

For information on career opportunities in commercial laboratories, contact:

National Association of Dental Laboratories, 3801 Mt. Vernon Ave., Alexandria, VA 22305.

Dispensing Optician

Job Description

After an eye examination by an ophthalmologist or an optometrist, people needing corrective lenses usually visit a dispensing optician to have the prescription filled. Optometrists generally fill prescriptions in-house. They may do their own dispensing or employ an optician to do it.

Dispensing opticians help customers select appropriate frames, order the necessary ophthalmic laboratory work, and adjust the finished eyeglasses. In some states, they fit contact lenses under the supervision of an optometrist or ophthalmologist.

Dispensing opticians examine written prescriptions to determine lens specifications. They then help the customer select from various styles and colors of eyeglass frames and lenses. The optician takes a number of measurements, including the distance between the centers of the pupils of the eyes to determine where the lens centers should be placed in relation to them and the distance between the eye surface and the lens. For the customer without a prescription, dispensing opticians may use a lensometer to record the customer's present eyeglass prescription. The dispensing optician then prepares a work order that gives the ophthalmic laboratory the information needed to grind and insert lenses into a frame.

Some dispensing opticians do their own laboratory work, preparing the lenses themselves. After the glasses are made, they check the optical center, power, and surface quality of the lenses with special instruments, then adjust the frame to the contours of the customer's face and head so that it fits properly and comfortably.

Almost half of dispensing opticians work for ophthalmologists or optometrists who sell glasses directly to patients. Many also work in optical shops or for department stores, drugstores, and other retail outlets.

Qualifications

Some firms hire individuals with no background in opticianry and train them on the job; others have taken courses in opticianry or completed a formal training program.

Solid math and science skills are important. Knowledge of physics, basic anatomy, algebra, geometry, and mechanical drawing is particularly valuable since training usually includes instruction in optical mathematics, optical physics, and the use of precision measuring instruments and other machinery and tools. Because dispensing opticians deal directly with the public, they should be tactful and pleasant and communicate well.

Some form of apprenticeship or formal traineeship is offered in most states. Large chain stores generally offer structured apprenticeship programs, whereas small companies provide more informal on-the-job training. Formal training in opticianry is also offered in community colleges.

Income and Advancement

The earnings of dispensing opticians vary greatly, depending on the size and location of the establishment where they work and the number of customers they serve. Those who work in states that require licensing and those who run their own stores often earn considerably more than those who do not. According to limited information, dispensing opticians average about $26,000 a year, their salaries ranging from about $20,990 to over $35,000 annually.

Many experienced dispensing opticians go into business for themselves. Others become managers of retail optical stores or sales representatives for wholesalers or manufacturers of eyeglasses or lenses.

Where to Get More Information

Opticians Association of America, 10341 Democracy Lane, P.O. Box 10110, Fairfax, VA 22030.

National Academy of Opticianry, 10111 Martin Luther King, Jr. Hwy., Bowie, MD 20720.

EEG Technologist

Job Description

"Brain waves" are electrical impulses that can be recorded by an electroencephalograph (EEG) machine. EEG technologists operate these machines. The tests performed with these machines help neurologists—physicians who study the brain—to diagnose brain tumors, strokes, and epilepsy; to measure the effects of infectious diseases on the brain; and to determine whether persons with mental or behavioral problems have an organic impairment, such as Alzheimer's disease. The tests are also used to determine the absence of brain activity, or "clinical" death, and to assess the probability of a recovery from a coma.

To produce the kind of record needed, EEG technologists apply electrodes on the patient's head by adjusting a combination of instrument controls. To record activity from both the central and peripheral nervous system, they also attach electrodes to the chest, arm, leg, or spinal column.

Technologists monitor the brain (and sometimes the heart) for 24 hours while patients carry out normal activities. After this period, they retrieve a small recorder that was carried by the patient. Then they obtain and review a readout from which they select the pertinent portions for study by a physician. They also administer sleep studies and perform EEGs to monitor and map brain wave activity to study abnormal sleep patterns.

Most technologists work in EEG or neurology laboratories of hospitals. Others work in offices of clinics of neurologists and neurosurgeons, health maintenance organizations, and psychiatric facilities.

Qualifications

EEG technologists generally learn their skills on the job, although some complete formal training programs. Applicants for trainee positions in hospitals need a high school diploma. Formal training is also offered in hospitals and community colleges. Programs usually last from one to two years and include laboratory experience as well as classroom instruction in neurology, anatomy, physiology, neurophysiology, electronics, and instrumentation. Graduates receive associate degrees or certificates.

Technologists should have manual dexterity, good vision, writing skills, an aptitude for working with electronic equipment, and the ability to work with patients and health care personnel. High school courses in health, biology, and mathematics are useful.

Income and Advancement

The median annual salary of EEG technologists in hospitals and medical centers, based on a 40-hour week and excluding shift or area differentials, is about $24,000. The average minimum salary is about $20,000, and the average maximum salary is about $28,900. EEG laboratory supervisors and training program directors generally earn higher salaries.

Technologists in large hospitals can advance to jobs in which they perform more difficult tests, then move up to the position of chief EEG technologist, in which they manage the laboratory. Chief EEG technologists generally are supervised by a physician, neurologist, or neurosurgeon. Technologists may also teach or go into research.

Where to Get More Information

Executive Office, American Society of Electroneurodiagnostic Technologists, Inc., 204 W. 7th St., Carroll, IA 51401.

Joint Review Committee on Electroneurodiagnostic Technology, P.O. Box 11434, Norfolk, VA 23517.

EKG Technician

Job Description

An electrocardiogram (EKG or ECG) measures the electrical impulses transmitted by the heart. EKG technicians operate electrocardiograph machines, which trace and record electrocardiograms.

EKGs help physicians diagnose heart disease, monitor the effect of drug therapy, and analyze changes in a patient's heart over time. An EKG test is done before most kinds of surgery and as part of a routine physical examination for persons past a certain age. EKG technicians attach electrodes to the patient's chest, arms, and legs. They then apply a gel or cream between the electrodes and the patient's skin to facilitate the passage of the electrical impulses. By manipulating switches on the electrocardiograph, technicians prepare electrocardiograms for analysis by a physician, usually a cardiologist, noting any abnormal readings.

Skilled EKG technicians perform ambulatory monitoring and stress testing. They place electrodes on the patient's chest and attach a portable EKG monitor to the patient's belt. Patients wear the monitor for 24 to 48 hours while pursuing their usual activities. Technicians then remove the electrodes and tape, place the tape in a scanner, and read it for electrical interference before sending it to a physician. Sometimes they prepare a report for the physician, noting any significant abnormalities.

For a treadmill stress test, technicians connect the patient to an EKG monitor, obtain a baseline reading, and test blood pressure. They have the patient walk on a treadmill, whose speed is gradually increased, under the supervision of a physician or nurse.

Most EKG technicians work in hospital cardiology departments. Some work in cardiologists' offices, cardiac rehabilitation centers, or health maintenance organizations.

Qualifications

Most EKG technicians are trained on the job. Applicants must be high school graduates, be reliable, have mechanical aptitude, and be able to follow detailed instructions. For those who want to learn basic EKG stress testing, one-year certificate programs exist. This is becoming a more common way to enter the field.

Income and Advancement

The median annual salary of EKG technicians, based on a 40-hour week and excluding shift and area differentials, is about $17,500; and the average maximum is about $22,000.

Where to Get More Information

Division of Allied Health Education and Accreditation Medical Association, 515 N. State St., Chicago, IL 60610.

The Society of Vascular Technology, 1101 Connecticut Ave., NW, Washington, DC 20036.

Local hospitals can supply information about employment opportunities.

Emergency Medical Technician

Job Description

Life-threatening emergencies demand urgent medical attention. When they occur, emergency medical technicians (EMTs) are there to give immediate care and then transport the sick or injured to medical facilities.

Following instructions from a dispatcher, EMTs drive specially equipped vehicles to the scene of an emergency. They determine the nature and extent of the patient's injuries or illness while also trying to determine whether the patient has preexisting medical conditions. EMTs then give appropriate emergency care, following strict guidelines for which procedures they may perform. All EMTs, including those with basic skills—the EMT Basics—may open airways, restore breathing, control bleeding, treat for shock, administer oxygen, bandage wounds, assist in childbirth, manage emotionally disturbed patients, treat and assist heart attack victims, and give initial care for poison and burn victims.

EMT-Intermediates, or EMT-Is, have more advanced training and can perform additional procedures, such as administering intravenous fluids or using a defibrillator to give life-saving shocks to a stopped heart.

EMT-Paramedics provide the most extensive prehospital care. They may administer drugs orally and intravenously, and they use monitors and other equipment. Complicated problems are carried out under step-by-step direction of medical personnel with whom the EMTs are in radio contact.

Two-fifths of EMTs work in private ambulance services; about a third work in municipal fire, police, or rescue squad departments; and a quarter work in hospitals. In addition, there are many volunteer EMTs.

Qualifications

Formal training is needed to become an EMT. An EMT-Basic requires 80 to 120 hours of classroom work plus 10 hours of internship in a hospital emergency room. Training is also offered the police, fire, and health departments; in hospitals; and as a nondegree course in colleges and universities. EMT-Intermediate training varies from state to state, but includes 35 to 55 hours of further instruction in patient assessment as well as the use of esophageal airways, intravenous fluids, and antishock garments. Training for EMT-Paramedics lasts between 750 and 2,000 hours. Refresher courses and continuing education are available for EMTs at all levels.

Applicants to an EMT training course generally must be at least 18 years old and have a high school diploma or the equivalent and a driver's license. High school subjects for prospective EMTs should include driver education, health, and science.

Income and Advancement

Earnings of EMTs depend on the employment setting and geographic location as well as the individual's training and experience. Average starting salaries in 1993 were $19,530 for EMT-Ambulance or EMT-Basic, $24,390 for EMT-Intermediate, and $25,050 for EMT-Paramedic. EMTs employed by fire departments earn the highest salaries, ranging from $30,914 to $34,994 per year.

Advancement beyond the EMT-Paramedic level usually means leaving fieldwork. An EMT-Paramedic can become a supervisor, an operations manager, an administrative director, or an executive director of emergency services. Some EMTs become instructors, firefighters, dispatchers, or police officers. Others move into sales or marketing of emergency medical equipment, all with opportunities for substantial increases in income. Finally, some become EMTs to assess their interest in health care and then decide to return to school and become RNs or physicians.

Where to Get More Information

Information concerning training courses, registration, and job opportunities for EMTs can be obtained by writing to your State Emergency Medical Service Director. General information about EMTs is available from:

National Association of Emergency Medical Technicians, 9140 Ward Pkwy., Kansas City, MO 64114.

Medical Records Technician

Job Description

When you enter a hospital, you are immediately aware of the whirl of white-coated physicians, nurses, and medical technologists of all stripes. What you are not aware of is the massive amount of paperwork that is produced daily. Every time a health care provider treats a patient, a record of the observations and treatment is made. This record includes information the patient provides about his or her symptoms and medical history, as well as the results of examinations, reports of X-ray and laboratory tests, and diagnoses and treatment plans. Medical records technicians organize and evaluate these records for completeness and accuracy.

When assembling a patient's medical record, technicians first make sure that the medical chart is complete, checking that all forms are present and properly identified and signed. Sometimes, they talk to physicians or others to clarify diagnoses or get additional information.

Technicians may use a packaged computer program to assign the patient to one of several hundred "diagnosis-related groups," or DRGs. The DRG determines the amount the hospital will be reimbursed if the patient is covered by Medicare or other insurance programs that use the DRG system.

Technicians may also tabulate and analyze data to help improve patient care, to control costs, to be used in legal actions, or to respond to surveys. Technicians known as "registrars" maintain registries showing occurrences of certain diseases.

Medical record technicians' duties vary with the size of the facility. In large to medium facilities, technicians may specialize in one aspect of medical records or supervise medical record clerks and transcriptionists, while a medical administrator manages the department.

The position of medical record technician is one of the few health occupations in which there is little or no contact with patients. Three out of five jobs are in hospitals. Most of the remainder are in nursing homes, medical group practices, health maintenance organizations, and clinics. Many insurance, accounting, and law firms that deal in health matters employ medical record technicians to tabulate and analyze data from medical records.

Qualifications

Medical record technicians entering the field usually have formal training in a two-year associate degree program offered at community and junior colleges. Courses include medical terminology and diseases, anatomy and physiology, legal aspects of medical records, coding and abstraction of data, statistics, databases, quality assurance methods, and computers.

Most employers prefer to hire accredited record technicians (ARTs). Accreditation is obtained by passing a written examination offered by the American Medical Record Association. To take the examination, a person must be a graduate of a two-year associate degree program.

Income and Advancement

Accredited record technicians who work as coders average $11.30 an hour. Those in supervisory positions average about $29,599 a year.

In large medical record departments, experienced technicians may become section supervisors, overseeing the work of the coding, correspondence, or discharge sections. A senior technician with Accredited Record Technician credentials may become director or assistant director of a medical record department in a small facility, with an accompanying increase in income and benefits.

Where to Get More Information

American Health Information Management Association, 919 Michigan Ave., Chicago, IL 60611.

American Medical Association, Division of Allied Health Education and Accreditation, 515 N. State St., Chicago, IL 60610.

Nuclear Medicine Technologist

Job Description

Nuclear medicine is the branch of radiology that uses unstable atoms, called "radionuclides," to diagnose and treat disease. Radionuclides are purified and compounded to form radiopharmaceuticals. These are then administered to patients and monitored to show the characteristics or functioning of those tissues or organs in which they localize. Abnormal areas show up as higher or lower concentrations of radioactivity than normal.

Nuclear medicine technologists perform these radioactive tests and procedures under the supervision of physicians. Technologists prepare and administer radiopharmaceuticals, then operate diagnostic imaging equipment that detects and maps the radioactive drug in the patient's body, to create an image.

Technologists first explain the test procedure to patients. Then nuclear medicine technologists calculate and prepare the correct dosage of the radiopharmaceutical and administer it by mouth, injection, or other means. Technologists position the patient and start the gamma scintillation camera, or "scanner," which creates images of the distribution of the radiopharmaceutical as it passes through or localizes in the patient's body. The images produced on a computer screen or on film are then interpreted by a physician.

Nuclear medicine technologists also perform clinical laboratory procedures called radioimmunoassay studies to assess the behavior of the radioactive substance inside the body instead of using a diagnostic image. Technologists ensure that radiation safety procedures are carefully followed by all workers in the nuclear medicine laboratory and that complete and accurate records are kept.

Nuclear medicine technologists may work evening or weekend hours in departments that operate on an extended schedule. Opportunities for part-time and shift work are also available. In addition, technologists in hospitals may be on-call on a rotational basis.

Qualifications

Nuclear medicine technology programs range in length from one to four years and may lead to a certificate, an associate degree, or a bachelor's degree. Generally, certificate programs are offered in hospitals; associate programs, in community colleges. Courses cover physical sciences, the biological effects of radiation exposure, radiation protection and procedures, radiopharmaceuticals and their use in patients, imaging techniques, and computer applications. Associate programs also cover liberal arts.

All nuclear medicine technologists must meet the minimum federal standards on the administration of radioactive drugs and the operation of radiologic equipment. About half of all states require technologists to be licensed.

Income and Advancement

The median salary for nuclear medicine technologists in hospitals and medical schools ranges from $32,843 to $38,840.

Technologists may advance to supervisor, then to chief technologist, and finally to department administrator or director. Some technologists specialize in a clinical area, such as nuclear cardiology or computer analysis, or they leave patient care to take positions in research laboratories. Some become instructors. Others leave the occupation to work as sales or training representatives with health equipment or radiopharmaceutical manufacturing firms. Some become radiation safety officers in regulatory agencies or hospitals, positions which build upon their background and experience.

Where to Get More Information

The Society of Nuclear Medicine Technologist Section, 136 Madison Ave., New York, NY 10016.

American Society of Radiologic Technologists, 15000 Central Ave., Albuquerque, NM 87123.

The American Registry of Radiologic Technologists, 1255 Northland Dr., Mendota Heights, MN 55120.

Nurse

Job Description

Nurses are persons who care for the sick, wounded, or enfeebled. Because nursing encompasses such widely diversified duties, it is divided into three major categories requiring different levels of education, training, and qualifications. They are licensed practical nurses (LPNs), nursing aides and psychiatric aides, and registered nurses (RNs).

Licensed Practical Nurse (LPN)

Job Description

Licensed practical nurses, or licensed vocational nurses (LVNs) as they are called in Texas and California, care for the sick, injured, convalescing, and handicapped, under the direction of physicians and registered nurses.

Most provide bedside care, monitoring such vital signs as temperature, blood pressure, pulse, and respiration. They prepare and give injections and enemas, apply dressings, give alcohol rubs and massages, apply ice packs and hot water bottles, and insert catheters. They help patients with bathing, dressing, and personal hygiene; feed them, and record food and liquid intake and output; and keep them comfortable.

LPNs in nursing homes, in addition to providing routine bedside care, may also help evaluate residents' needs, develop care plans, and supervise nursing aides. In doctors' offices and clinics, they may also make appointments, keep records, and perform other clerical duties. LPNs who work in home health may also prepare meals and teach family members simple nursing tasks.

About a quarter of LPNs work part-time. Almost half work in hospitals, almost one-quarter work in nursing homes, and a tenth work in doctors' offices and clinics. Others work for temporary help agencies, home health care services, or government agencies.

Qualifications

All states require LPNs to pass a licensing examination after completing a state-approved practical nursing program. A high school diploma is usually required for entry, but some programs accept people who have completed less.

Trade, technical, or vocational schools offer almost half of these programs, whereas community and junior colleges provide more than a third. Some programs are offered in high schools, hospitals, and colleges. Most practical nursing programs last about one year and include both classroom study and clinical practice. Classroom study covers basic nursing concepts and related subjects, including anatomy, physiology, medical-surgical nursing, pediatrics, obstetrics, psychiatric nursing, administration of drugs, nutrition, and first aid. Supervised clinical experience is usually in a hospital but sometimes also includes other settings.

LPNs should have a caring, sympathetic nature. They should be emotionally stable because work with the sick and injured can be stressful.

Income and Advancement

Annual earnings of LPNs who work full time range from $21,476 to $25,948, with the top 10 percent earning more than $51,668.

Where to Get More Information

Communications Department, National League for Nursing, 350 Hudson St., New York, NY 10014.

National Association for Practical Nurse Education and Service, Inc., 1400 Spring St., Silver Spring, MD 20910.

National Federation of Licensed Practical Nurses, Inc., P.O. Box 18048, Raleigh, NC 27619.

Nursing Aide and Psychiatric Aide

Job Description

Nursing aides and psychiatric aids help care for physically or mentally ill, injured, disabled, or infirm individuals confined to hospitals, nursing or residential care facilities, and mental health settings.

Nursing aides, also known as nursing assistants or hospital attendants, work under the supervision of nursing and medical staff. They answer patients' call bells; deliver messages; serve meals; make beds; and feed, dress, and bathe patients. Aides may also take temperatures, pulse, respiration, and blood pressure, and help patients get in and out of bed and walk. They may also escort patients to operating and examination rooms, keep patients' rooms neat, set up equipment, or store and move supplies. Aides observe patients' physical, mental, and emotional conditions and report any change to the nursing or medical staff. Nursing aides are often the principal caregivers in nursing homes.

Psychiatric aides are also known as mental health assistants, psychiatric nursing assistants, or ward attendants. They care for mentally impaired or emotionally disturbed individuals. They work under a team that may include psychiatrists, psychologists, psychiatric nurses, social workers, and therapists. They observe patients and report any signs that might be important for the professional staff to know about.

Nursing aides often have to empty bedpans, change soiled bed linens, and care for disoriented and irritable patients. Psychiatric aides are often confronted with violent patients. While the work can be emotionally draining, many aides gain satisfaction from assisting those in need.

About one-half of all nursing aides work in nursing homes, and about one-fourth work in hospitals. Some work in residential care facilities or in private households. Most psychiatric aides work in state and county mental institutions, psychiatric units of general hospitals, private psychiatric facilities, community mental health centers, residential facilities for the developmentally disabled, halfway houses, and drug abuse and alcoholism treatment programs.

Qualifications

In many cases, neither a high school diploma nor previous work experience is necessary for a job as a nursing or psychiatric aide. Some employers, however, require some training or experience.

Nursing aide training is offered in high schools, vocational-technical centers, many nursing homes, and community colleges. Courses cover body mechanics, nutrition, anatomy, physiology, infection control, and communications skills.

Applicants should be healthy, tactful, patient, understanding, emotionally stable, and dependable, and have a desire to help people.

Income and Advancement

Median annual earnings of nursing and psychiatric aides range from $11,500 to $17,900. The top 10 percent earn $23,900 or more. Paid holidays and sick leave, hospital and medical benefits, extra pay for late-shift work, and pension plans are available to many hospital and nursing-home employees.

Applicants may be able to enter other health occupations but generally need additional formal training. Some employers and unions provide opportunities for transfer into other health care occupations with more responsibility and higher salaries.

Where to Get More Information

American Health Care Association, 1201 L St., Washington, DC, 20005.

Registered Nurse (RN)

Job Description

Registered nurses are typically concerned with the "whole person," providing for the physical, mental, and emotional needs of their patients. They observe, assess, and record symptoms, reactions, and progress. They assist physicians, administer medications, assist in convalescence and rehabilitation, instruct patients and their families in proper care, and help individuals and groups take steps to improve or maintain their health.

Hospital nurses form the largest group of nurses. Most are staff nurses who provide bedside nursing care and carry out the medical regimen prescribed by physicians. They may also supervise licensed practical nurses and aides. Hospital nurses usually are assigned to one area, such as surgery, maternity, pediatrics, emergency room, or intensive care; or they may rotate among departments.

Nursing-home nurses work in government and private agencies and clinics, schools, retirement communities, and other community settings. They work with community leaders, teachers, parents, and physicians in community health education. Some work in home health care, providing periodic services prescribed by physicians and instructing patients and families.

Private-duty nurses care for patients needing constant attention. They work directly for families on a contract basis or for a nursing or temporary help agency that assigns them to patients.

Office nurses assist physicians in private practice, clinics, emergency medical centers, and health maintenance organizations (HMOs). They prepare patients for and help with examinations, administer injections and medications, dress wounds, assist with minor surgery, and maintain records.

Occupational health or industrial nurses provide nursing care at worksites, to employees, customers, and others with minor injuries and illnesses.

About two out of three registered nurses work in hospitals. Others are in offices of physicians, nursing homes, temporary help agencies, schools, and government agencies. About one-fourth of all RNs work part-time.

Qualifications

To obtain a nursing license, all states require graduation from an accredited nursing school and a passing grade on a national licensing examination. There are three major educational paths to nursing: an associate degree (ADN), a diploma, and a bachelor of science degree in nursing (BSN). ADN programs, offered by community and junior colleges, take about two years. BSN programs, offered by colleges and universities, take four or five years, and diploma programs, given in hospitals, last two or three years. Generally, licensed graduates of any of the three programs qualify for entry-level positions as staff nurses. Because many hospitals have tuition reimbursement programs, individuals with limited resources can get a two-year degree, find a hospital position, and let their employer finance a four-year BSN degree.

Income and Advancement

Based on 40 hours a week, median annual earnings of registered nurses employed full time in private hospitals are about $35,000, excluding premium pay for overtime and for work on weekends, holidays, and late shifts. Top earnings can reach more than $51,000. Nurse anesthetists can earn about $66,622 a year.

Within patient care, advancement may mean becoming a clinical nurse specialist, nurse practitioner, nurse clinician, nurse midwife, or nurse anesthetist. For these positions, additional education or training is required.

Some nurses move into the business side of health care. Their nursing expertise and experience on a health care team equip them to manage ambulatory, acute, home health, and chronic care services. Some are employed by health care corporations in health planning and development, marketing, and quality assurance.

Where to Get More Information

Communications Department, National League for Nursing, 350 Hudson St., New York, NY 10014.

American Nurses' Association, 600 Maryland Ave., SW, Washington, DC 20024.

American Health Care Association, 1201 L St., NW, Washington, DC 20005.

Radiologic Technologist

Job Description

Medical uses of radiation go far beyond the diagnosis of broken bones. Radiation is used not only to produce images of the interior of the body but to treat cancer as well. Imaging techniques that do not involve X-rays embrace such procedures as ultrasound and magnetic resonance as well as the familiar X-ray.

Radiographers produce X-ray films, called radiographs, of parts of the human body and use these films to diagnose problems. Radiographers position radiographic equipment at the correct angle and height over the appropriate area of a patient's body, then set controls on the machine to produce radiographs. Technologists then remove the film and develop it.

Experienced radiographers may perform more complex imaging tests—for instance, fluoroscopies, which allow the physician to see soft tissues in the body. They also take tomography scans (CTs) by using a computer to enhance the X-ray. For magnetic resonance imaging (MRI), technologists use giant magnets and radio waves to create an image.

Radiation therapy technologists prepare cancer patients for treatment and administer doses of ionizing radiation to specific parts of the body. Technologists also operate many kinds of equipment, including high-energy electron linear accelerators.

Sonographers, or ultrasound technologists, use ultrasound equipment to transmit high-frequency sound waves into areas of the patient's body in order to produce reflected echoes that form an image which can be viewed on a screen, recorded on a printout strip, or photographed for use in interpretation and diagnosis by a physician.

About three out of five jobs are with hospitals. The rest are in physicians' offices, clinics, and diagnostic imaging centers.

Qualifications

Preparation for this field is available in hospitals, colleges and universities, and vocational and technical schools. Hospitals provide employment for most radiologic technologists, and they prefer to hire those with some formal training.

Programs range in length from one to four years and lead to a certificate, an associate degree, or a bachelor's degree. Two-year programs are the most common. Some one-year programs are available for those who are in other health occupations, such as medical technologists and registered nurses who want to change fields.

Radiography programs require a high school diploma or equivalent. High school courses in mathematics, physics, chemistry, and biology are helpful. For training programs in radiation therapy and diagnostic medical sonography, applicants with either a background in science or experience in one of the health professions generally are preferred.

Income and Advancement

The median annual earnings for full-time radiologic technologists who work year-round are about $28,350. The middle 50 percent earn between $23,000 and $33,748 a year, whereas the highest-paid 10 percent earn more than $40,500.

With experience and additional training, staff technologists in large radiography departments may be promoted to clinical jobs in which they perform special procedures, including CT scanning, ultrasound, angiography, and magnetic resonance imaging. They also may be promoted to supervisory positions, such as supervisor, chief technologist, or department administrator or director.

Where to Get More Additional Information

American Society of Radiologic Technologists, 15000 Central Ave., SE, Albuquerque, NM 87123.

Society of Diagnostic Medical Sonographers, 12770 Coit Rd., Dallas, TX 75231.

Division of Allied Health Education and Accreditation, American Medical Association, 515 N. State St., Chicago, IL 60610.

Surgical Technologist

Job Description

Surgical technologists, or operating room technicians, assist in operations under the supervision of surgeons or registered nurses. They help set up the operating room with surgical instruments, equipment, sterile linens and other necessary equipment and materials. They check nonsterile equipment to ensure that it is in working order. Technologists also "prep" (prepare patients) for surgery by washing, shaving, and disinfecting incision sites. They transport patients to the operating room, help position them on the operating table, and cover them with sterile surgical "drapes."

During surgery, surgical technologists pass instruments and other sterile supplies to surgeons and surgeon assistants. They may operate sterilizers, lights, or suction machines, and help operate diagnostic equipment.

Qualifications

Surgical technologists receive training in formal programs offered by community and junior colleges, vocational schools, universities, and hospitals. Programs last nine to 24 months and lead to a certificate, a diploma, or an associate degree.

Required study includes anatomy, physiology, microbiology, pharmacology, and medical terminology. Students also learn to sterilize instruments; prevent and control infection; and handle special drugs, solutions, and equipment.

Income and Advancement

According to available information, the median annual salary of surgical technologists, based on a 40-hour week and excluding shift or area differential, was $21,741 in 1992, with the average maximum salary averaging about $26,480. Salaries vary according to the technologist's specialty and the size of the medical facility and its geographical location.

Technologists may advance by specializing in a particular area of surgery, such as neurosurgery or open-heart surgery. They may also work as circulating technologists. They may manage central supply departments in hospitals or take positions with insurance companies, sterile supply services, or operating equipment firms.

Where to Get More Information

Association of Surgical Technologists, 7108-CS Alton Way, Englewood, CO 80112.

Physician Assistant

Job Description

Physician assistants (PAs) are formally trained to perform many of the routine tasks physicians usually do. They take medical histories, examine patients, order laboratory tests, and make preliminary diagnoses. They also treat minor injuries, counsel patients, and order and carry out therapy. In 35 states and the District of Columbia, they may prescribe medications.

PAs always work under the supervision of a physician. In rural or inner-city clinics, where a doctor may be available for just one or two days a week, PAs may provide most of the health care for patients and consult with the supervising physician by telephone.

Most PAs work in physicians' offices and clinics. Others work in hospitals. The rest work for public health clinics, nursing homes, prisons, and rehabilitation centers.

Qualifications

Almost all states require that new PAs complete an accredited education program. Admission requirements vary, but many programs require two years of college and some work experience in the health care field. Students take courses in biology, English, chemistry, math, psychology, and social sciences. Many applicants are former emergency medical technicians, other allied health professionals, or nurses.

PA programs generally last two years. These programs are located in medical schools, schools of allied health, four-year colleges, community colleges, or hospitals. PA education includes classroom instruction in biochemistry, nutrition, human anatomy, physiology, microbiology, clinical pharmacology, clinical medicine, geriatric and home health care, disease prevention, and medical ethics.

Physicians assistants need leadership skills, self-confidence, and emotional stability. They must be willing to continue studying throughout their career to keep up with medical advances.

Income and Advancement

According to the American Academy of Physician Assistants, the average salary for all PAs in 1993 was between $50,000 and $55,000. Salaries vary according to specialty, practice setting, geographical location, education, and years of experience.

Where to Get More Information

American Academy of Physician Assistants, 950 N. Washington St., Alexandria, VA 22314.

HOSPITALITY, TRAVEL, AND FOOD SERVICES

· ·

Chef

Job Description

The key to the success of any restaurant is the training and skill of the chef. Restaurants may offer a varied menu featuring meals that are time-consuming and difficult to prepare, requiring a highly skilled chef. Others may emphasize fast service, offering meals that can be prepared in advance.

Chefs are responsible for preparing meals that are tasty and attractively presented. Many chefs have earned fame for both themselves and the restaurants, hotels, and institutions where they work because of their skill in artfully preparing the traditional favorites, creating new dishes, or producing examples of exotic foreign cuisine.

Institutional chefs work in the kitchens of schools, industrial cafeterias, hospitals, and other institutions. Restaurant chefs generally prepare a wider selection of dishes for each meal, cooking most individual servings to order. Whether in institutions or restaurants, chefs measure, mix, and cook ingredients according to recipes. They are often responsible for estimating food requirements and ordering food supplies. Some chefs help plan meals and develop menus. Large operations often employ several chefs, sometimes called assistant or apprentice chefs.

Qualifications

Even though a high school diploma is not required for beginning jobs, it is recommended for those planning a career as a chef. High school or vocational school courses in business arithmetic and business administration are particularly helpful.

An increasing number of chefs obtain their training through high school or post–high school vocational programs. Chefs may also be trained in apprenticeship programs offered by professional culinary institutes, industry associations, and trade unions. An example is the three-year apprenticeship program administered by local chapters of the American Culinary Federation in cooperation with local employers and junior colleges or vocational education institutions. In addition, some large hotels and restaurants operate their own training programs for chefs.

The ability to work as part of a team, a keen sense of taste and smell, and personal cleanliness are important qualifications for chefs. Advancement depends not only on culinary skills but on ability to supervise lesser-skilled workers and limit food costs by minimizing waste and accurately anticipating the amount of perishable supplies needed.

Income and Advancement

Most chefs start out as cooks at relatively low wages. With specialized training and experience, they can advance to executive positions or management positions, particularly in hotels, clubs, or larger and more elegant restaurants. Some eventually go into business as caterers or restaurant owners.

The wages of chefs depend on the part of the country and, especially, the type of establishment, in which they work. Salaries generally are highest in elegant restaurants and hotels. Executive chefs earn $40,000 per year or more, and some chefs employed by internationally famous hotels and restaurants earn in excess of $75,000.

Where to Get More Information

The Educational Foundation of the National Restaurant Association, 250 S. Wacker Drive, Chicago, IL 60606.

American Culinary Federation, P.O. Box 3466, St. Augustine, FL 32085.

Council on Hotel, Restaurant and Institutional Education, 1200 17th St., NW, Washington, DC 20036.

Flight Attendant

Job Description

Flight attendants look after airline passengers' safety and comfort. They serve aboard almost all passenger planes. Before each flight, the captain briefs attendants on such things as expected weather conditions and special passenger problems. The attendants see that the passenger cabin is in order; that supplies of food, beverages, blankets, and reading material are adequate; and that first-aid kits and other emergency equipment are aboard and in working order. As passengers board the plane, the attendants greet them, check their tickets, and assist them in storing coats and carry-on luggage.

Before takeoff, flight attendants instruct passengers in the use of emergency equipment and check to see that all passengers have their seat belts fastened. They distribute magazines and pillows, help care for small children and elderly and handicapped persons, and answer questions about the flight. Attendants also serve cocktails and other refreshments and, on many flights, heat and distribute precooked meals. After the plane has landed, they assist passengers leaving the plane.

Helping passengers in the rare event of an emergency is the most important function of attendants. They may range from reassuring passengers during occasional encounters with strong turbulence, to opening emergency exits and inflating evacuation chutes following an emergency landing.

Because airlines operate year-round and around-the-clock, attendants may work at night and on holidays and weekends. They usually fly 75 to 85 hours a month; and they spend about 75 to 85 hours a month on the ground, preparing planes for flight and writing reports following completed trips. Because of variations in scheduling and limitations on flying time, many attendants have 11 or more days off each month. They may be away from their home bases at least one-third of the time. During this period, the airlines provide hotel accommodations and an allowance for meal expenses.

Qualifications

The airlines prefer poised, tactful, and resourceful people who can deal comfortably with strangers. Applicants usually must be at least 19 to 21 years old, but some airlines have higher minimum-age requirements.

Applicants must be high school graduates. Those having some experience in dealing with the public are preferred. Flight attendants for international airlines generally must speak an appropriate foreign language fluently.

Most large airlines required that newly hired flight attendants complete four to six weeks of intensive training in their own schools. Trainees learn such emergency procedures as operating an oxygen system and giving first aid. They also are taught flight regulations and duties, and company operations and policies. Trainees receive instruction on personal grooming and weight control. Those selected for international routes get additional instruction in passport and customs regulations. Towards the end of their training, students go on practice flights. They must receive 12 to 14 hours of training in emergency procedures and passenger relations annually.

After completing training, flight attendants are assigned to one of their airline's bases. New attendants are placed in "reserve status" and are called on either to staff extra flights or to fill in for attendants who are sick or on vacation. Attendants usually remain on reserve for one or more years.

Income and Advancement

Beginning flight attendants have median earnings of about $13,000 a year, according to data from the Association of Flight Attendants. Flight attendants with six years of flying experience have median annual earnings of about $20,000, while some senior flight attendants earn $40,000 a year. Flight attendants receive extra compensation for overtime and for night and international flights. In addition, they and their immediate families are entitled to reduced fares on the airline they work for, as well as on most other airlines.

Many flight attendants belong to the Association of Flight Attendants. Others are members of the Transport Workers of America or several other unions. Some attendants transfer to flight service instructor, customer service director, recruiting representative, or various other administrative positions.

Where to Get More Information

Information about job opportunities in a particular airline and the qualifications required may be obtained by writing to the personnel manager of the company. For addresses of airline companies and information about job opportunities and salaries, contact:

Future Aviation Professionals of America, 4959 Massachusetts Blvd., Atlanta, GA 30337. (This organization may be called toll-free at 800-Jet-Jobs.)

Hotel Manager and Assistant

Job Description

Vacationers and business travelers find a welcome haven at hotels and motels across the nation. A comfortable room, good food, and a helpful hotel staff can make being away from home an enjoyable experience. Whether you stay overnight at a roadside motel, spend several days at a towering downtown convention hotel, or stay a week at a large resort complex with a variety of recreational facilities, your comfort is in the hands of the hotel manager and assistant manager.

Hotel managers are responsible for the efficient and profitable operation of their establishments. In a small hotel, a motel, or an inn with a limited staff, a single manager may direct all aspects of operations. Large hotels, however, may employ hundreds of workers, and the manager may be aided by a number of assistant managers.

General managers have overall responsibility for the operation of the hotel. They usually set room rates, allocate funds to departments, approve expenditures, and establish decor, housekeeping, food quality, and banquet operations.

Resident managers live in hotels and are on-call 24 hours a day to resolve any problems or emergencies, although they normally work an eight-hour day. The most senior assistant manager oversees the day-to-day operations of the hotel.

Executive housekeepers are responsible for ensuring that guest rooms, meeting and banquet rooms, and public areas are clean, orderly, and well-maintained. They train, schedule, and supervise the work of housekeepers, inspect rooms, and order cleaning supplies.

Front-office managers coordinate reservations and room assignments and train and direct the hotel's front-desk staff that deals with the public. They ensure that guests are handled courteously and efficiently, resolve complaints, and request special services when required.

Food and beverage managers direct the food service of hotels. They oversee the operation of hotel restaurants, cocktail lounges, and banquet facilities. They supervise and schedule food and beverage preparation and service workers' duties, plan menus, estimate costs, and deal with food suppliers.

Convention services managers coordinate the activities of large hotels' various departments for meetings, conventions, and other special events. They meet with representatives of groups or organizations to plan the number of rooms to reserve, the amount of hotel meeting space required, and any banquet services needed.

Qualifications

Training in hotel or restaurant management is preferred for most hotel management positions. Some persons still advance from the ranks of front-desk clerks, housekeepers, waiters, and chefs, without the benefit of education or training beyond high school, but, increasingly, some specialized education is preferred. Still, experience working in a hotel—even part-time while in school—is an asset for applicants seeking to enter hotel management careers.

More than 800 community and junior colleges, technical institutes, and vocational and trade schools have programs leading to an associate degree or other formal recognition in hotel or restaurant management. Graduates of these programs usually start as trainee assistant managers, or they advance to such positions more quickly.

Hotel managers must be able to get along with all kinds of people. They need initiative, self-discipline, and the ability to organize and direct the work of others. They must be able to solve problems and concentrate on details.

Some large hotels sponsor specialized on-the-job management training programs that enable trainees to rotate among various departments and gain a thorough knowledge of hotel operations.

Income and Advancement

Salaries of hotel managers vary greatly according to the manager's responsibilities and the size of the hotel in which he or she works. Annual salaries of assistant hotel managers average about $32,500. Assistants employed in large hotels with more than 350 rooms average nearly $38,500, whereas those in small hotels with no more than 150 rooms average less than $26,000. Food and beverage managers average $41,200; front-office managers, $26,500.

Salaries of general managers average more than $59,100, ranging from an average of about $44,900 in hotels and motels with no more than 150 rooms, to an average of about $86,700 in large hotels with more than 350 rooms. Managers may earn bonuses of up to 15 percent of their basic salary in some hotels. In addition, they and their families may be furnished with lodging, meals, parking, laundry, and other services.

Where to Get More Information

The American Hotel and Motel Association (AH&MA), Information Center, 1201 New York Ave., NW, Washington, DC 20005.

The Educational Institute of AH&MA, P.O. Box 1240, East Lansing, MI 48826.

National Executive Housekeepers Association, Inc., 1001 Eastwind Dr., Westerville, OH 43081.

For information on hospitality careers, and a directory of colleges and other schools offering programs and courses in hotel and restaurant administration, write to:

Council on Hotel, Restaurant, and Institutional Education, 1200 17th St., NW, Washington, DC 20036

Restaurant and Food Service Manager

Job Description

There are probably as many different kinds of eating places in America as there are tastes. Choices range from restaurants that serve fast food to those that emphasize elegant dining. In addition, there are dining services in school and employee cafeterias, hospitals, and nursing facilities. The cuisine offered, its price, and the setting in which it is consumed vary greatly, but the managers of these diverse facilities have many responsibilities in common.

Efficient and profitable management of all of them require that managers and assistant managers select and appropriately price menu items, achieve consistent quality in food preparation and service, recruit and train workers and supervise their work, and attend to the various administrative aspects of the business.

In most restaurants and institutional food service facilities, the manager is assisted by one or more assistant managers, depending on the size and business hours of the establishment. In fast-food restaurants and other service facilities that operate long hours, seven days a week, the manager and assistant manager supervise a shift of workers. They work with chefs to select menu items; analyze the recipes of the dishes to determine food, labor, and overhead costs; and assign prices to the menu items.

On a daily basis, managers order supplies and deal with suppliers, estimate food consumption, place orders with vendors, and schedule the delivery of fresh food and beverages. They check the content of deliveries, evaluating the quality of meats, poultry, fish, fruits, vegetables, and baked goods. Managers meet or talk with sales representatives of restaurant suppliers to place orders to replenish tableware, linens, paper, cleaning supplies, cooking utensils, and furniture and fixtures.

Restaurant and food managers oversee food preparation and cooking, checking food quality and portion sizes and ensuring that dishes are prepared correctly and in a timely manner.

Qualifications

Many restaurant and food service manager positions are filled by promoting experienced food and beverage preparation and service workers. Waiters, waitresses, chefs, and fast-food workers who have demonstrated their potential for handling responsibility can advance to assistant manager or management trainee jobs.

Programs in restaurant and food service occupations are offered by more than 800 community and junior colleges, technical institutes, and other institutions, leading to a two-year associate degree or certificate. They provide instruction in accounting, business law and management, food planning and preparation, and nutrition. Some programs combine classroom and laboratory study with internships that provide on-the-job experience.

Job applicants need self-discipline, initiative, and leadership ability, as well as good communication skills. Most restaurant chains and food service management companies provide rigorous training programs for persons hired for management jobs, through a combination of classroom and on-the-job training.

Income and Advancement

Earnings of restaurant and food service managers vary greatly according to the type and size of the establishment. Their median base salary was about $27,900 a year in 1993. Managers of the largest restaurants and institutional food service facilities often have annual salaries in excess of $45,000. Managers of fast-food restaurants have a median base salary of about $24,900, whereas managers of full-menu restaurants with table service and managers of commercial and institutional cafeterias earn about $29,500 to $31,000 a year. Besides a salary, most receive an annual bonus or incentive payment based on their performance. Assistant managers earnings range from $21,000 to over $31,000 a year.

Managers advance to larger establishments or to regional management positions with restaurant chains. Some eventually open their own eating and drinking establishments. Others transfer to hotel management positions as food and beverage managers in hotels and resorts.

Where to Get More Information

The Educational Foundation of the National Restaurant Association, 250 S. Wacker Dr., Chicago, IL 60606.

Council on Hotel, Restaurant, and Institutional Education, 1200 17th St., NW, Washington, DC 20036.

Travel Agent

Job Description

You need only observe the activities at any airport, railroad, bus, or steamship terminal to come to the conclusion that the entire population seems to be on the move 24 hours a day.

A major force behind transportation companies, hotels, motels, and resorts is the travel agent. According to the needs of the client, travel agents give advice on destinations; make arrangements for transportation, hotel accommodations, car rentals, tours, and recreation; or plan the right vacation package or business/pleasure trip combination. They may also give advice on restaurants, tourist attractions, and recreation. For international travel, agents also provide information on customs regulations, required papers (passports, visas, and certificates of vaccination), and currency exchange rates. Travel agents may also plan conventions and other meetings.

Travel agents consult a variety of published and computer-based sources for information on departure and arrival times, fares, and hotel ratings and accommodations. They often base recommendations on their own travel experiences or those of colleagues or clients. Travel agents may visit hotels, resorts, and restaurants to judge, firsthand, their comfort, cleanliness, and quality of food and service.

More than nine out of ten agents work for travel agencies; some work for membership organizations. Many travel agents are self-employed. Nearly one-half of the travel agencies are in suburban areas; about 40 percent are in large cities; and the rest, in small towns and rural areas.

Qualifications

In most instances a college education is not a prerequisite for employment as a travel agent. Many employers, however, look for some formal or specialized training for entry into the field. Many vocational schools offer three- to twelve-week full-time programs, as well as evening and Saturday programs. Travel courses are also offered in public adult education programs and two-year community colleges. Several home-study courses provide a basic understanding of the travel industry. The American Society of Travel Agents (ASTA) and the Institute of Certified Travel Agents offer a travel correspondence course. Travel agencies also provide on-the-job training for their employees. Today, employers in almost every field require computer skills, and these are especially necessary in the travel agency business where arrangements and reservations are made through computerized networks. A significant part of training programs consists of computer instruction.

Travel experience is an asset since personal knowledge about a city or foreign country often helps to influence clients' travel plans. Travel agents need good selling skills. They must be pleasant and patient and able to gain the confidence of customers. Some people start as reservations clerks or receptionists in travel agencies. With experience and some formal training, they can take on greater responsibilities and eventually assume travel agent duties.

Income and Advancement

A travel agent's sales ability and experience and the size and location of the agency determine his or her salary. Earnings of experienced travel agents range from about $16,000 to $27,000 or more a year. Managers of large travel agencies offices can earn considerably more.

In addition to salaries, many travel agencies offer extra income in the form of commissions for bringing in new business. Perks in the travel agency business include free or heavily discounted travel on airlines and other carriers and free accommodations in hotels and vacation resorts. Many travel agency employees are able to open their own agencies after learning the business and developing contacts for potential clients.

Where to Get More Information

American Society of Travel Agents (ASTA), 1101 King St., Alexandria, VA 22314.

The Institute of Certified Travel Agents, 148 Lindon St., Wellesley, MA 02181.

INDUSTRIAL PRODUCTION AND PRINTING

●●●

Bindery Worker

Job Description

Binding is the process of combining printed sheets of books, magazines, catalogs, folders, or directories. It involves cutting, folding, gathering, gluing, stitching, trimming, sewing, wrapping, and other finishing operations. Bindery workers operate the machines that perform these various tasks.

The duties of bindery worker vary according to what is being bound. For example, workers may bind books produced in large numbers, or "runs." Job binders bind books produced in smaller quantities. In companies that specialize in library binding, workers repair books and provide other specialized binding services to libraries. Pamphlet binders produce leaflets and folders, and manifold binders bind business forms. Blank bookbinders bind blank pages to produce notebooks, checkbooks, address books, diaries, calendars, and note pads.

Books and magazines are assembled from large, flat, printed sheets of paper. Skilled bookbinders operate machines that first fold the sheets into units known as "signatures," which are groups of pages arranged sequentially. Bookbinders then stitch or glue the assembled signatures together, use presses and trimming machines to shape the book, and reinforce them with glued fabric strips. Covers are created separately and glued, pasted, or stitched onto the book bodies.

A small number of bookbinders work in hand binderies. These highly skilled workers design original or special bindings for limited editions, or they restore rare books.

Qualifications

Employers usually prefer high school graduates. Finger dexterity is essential, and mechanical aptitude is needed to operate the newer automated equipment. Artistic ability and imagination are necessary for hand bookbinding.

Most workers learn the craft through on-the-job training, where they learn basic binding skills, including the characteristics of paper. As they gain experience, they advance to more difficult tasks and learn how to operate one or more pieces of equipment. High school students interested in bindery careers can gain exposure to the craft by taking shop courses or attending a vocational-technical high school.

Formal apprenticeships provide more structured programs that enable workers to acquire the high levels of specialization and skill needed. Training in graphic arts is also an asset. Postsecondary programs in the graphic arts are offered by vocational-technical institutes or at community and junior colleges.

Income and Advancement

The median income of skilled bookbinders ranges from about $300 to $480 a week, while the highest-paid workers earn $650 a week or more. Workers covered by union contracts generally have higher earnings and better fringe benefits.

Where to Get More Information

Education Council of the Graphic Arts Industry, 1899 Preston White Dr., Reston, VA 22091.

Graphic Communications International Union, 1900 L St., NW, Washington, DC 20036.

Industrial Production Manager

Job Description

Industrial production managers coordinate the many aspects of industrial production and direct the work of first-line supervisors. Because few factories are exactly alike, managers' duties may vary from plant to plant. Regardless of the industry, however, they generally have the same major functions. These include responsibility for production scheduling, staffing, equipment, quality control, inventory control, and the coordination of activities with other departments.

Production managers usually report to the plant manager or the vice president for manufacturing. In many plants, one production manager is responsible for all production. In large plants with several operations, there are managers in charge of each operation, such as machining, assembly, or finishing.

Production managers plan the production schedule, analyze the plant's personnel and capital resources, and select the best way to meet the production quota. They determine which machines will be used, monitor the production run to make sure that it stays on schedule, and take action to solve problems when they occur. They work closely with other departments to plan and implement the company's goals and policies.

Most industrial production managers divide their time between the shop floor and their office. In facilities that operate around the clock, managers may have to work shifts or may be called at any hour to deal with emergencies that could result in production-line downtime.

Although employed throughout manufacturing, about one-half of industrial production managers are employed in five industries: industrial machinery and equipment, transportation equipment, fabricated metal products, food products, and chemicals.

Qualifications

Because manufacturing operations and job requirements are so diverse, there is no standard preparation for this occupation. Some industrial production managers have a college degree in business administration or industrial engineering, but many are former production-line workers who have been promoted through the ranks. Blue-collar workers who advance to production managers positions already have an intimate knowledge of the production process and the firm's organization. These workers must have demonstrated leadership ability and often take company-sponsored courses in management skills and communications techniques.

Income and Advancement

Salaries of industrial production managers vary significantly by industry and plant size. Annual salaries range from $60,000 in the smallest establishment to $85,000 in the largest. In addition, managers usually receive bonuses based on job performance.

Industrial production managers with a proven record of superior performance may advance to the position of plant manager or vice president for manufacturing. Others transfer to jobs at larger firms and acquire more responsibilities and increased income.

Where to Get More Information

American Production & Inventory Control Society, 500 W. Annandale Rd., Falls Church, VA 22046.

Institute of Industrial Engineers, 25 Technology Park/Atlanta, Norcross, GA 30092.

American Management Associations, 135 W. 50th St., New York, NY 10020.

Jeweler

Job Description

Jewelry made from precious metals and stones, such as gold and diamonds, has been worn by people for thousands of years. Jewelers use these materials to make, repair, and adjust rings, necklaces, bracelets, earrings, and other jewelry, using a variety of tools and materials.

Jewelers may specialize in one or more areas—buying, design, gem cutting, repair, sales, or appraisal. Typical work includes enlarging or reducing rings, resetting stones, and replacing broken clasps and mountings. Some jewelers also design or make their own jewelry by shaping the metal they have chosen or by carving wax to make a model for casting the metal. The jeweler then solders together the individual parts and may mount a diamond or other stone or may engrave a design into the metal.

Jewelers in retail stores are primarily involved in sales. Many are qualified gemologists who appraise the quality and value of diamonds, other gemstones, and gem materials.

In manufacturing, jewelers usually specialize in a single operation. Some jewelers may make models or tools for the jewelry that is to be produced. Others do finishing work, such as setting stones or engraving. Lasers are often used for cutting and improving the quality of stones. Some jewelers use computers to design and create customized pieces according to customers' wishes.

In repair shops, jewelers generally work alone with little supervision. In retail stores, however, they may talk with customers about repairs, perform custom design work, and do some sales work.

Over two-fifths of all jewelers are self-employed. Many operate their own store or repair shop, and some specialize in designing and creating custom jewelry. About half of all salaried jewelers work in retail establishments, whereas approximately one-third are employed in manufacturing.

Qualifications

For those interested in working in a jewelry store or repair shop, technical schools or courses offered by local colleges are the best sources of training. These programs vary in length from six months to two years. Students learn the use of jeweler's tools and machines and basic jewelry making and repairs skills. Technical school courses also cover blueprint reading, math, and shop theory. Most employers feel that graduates need additional on-the-job training to refine their repair skills and to learn more about the operation of the store or shop.

Technical school programs (which last about six months) and correspondence courses also offer training in gemology and appraising. These programs cover a wide range of topics, including evaluating diamonds and colored stones, identifying gems, and designing jewelry.

In jewelry manufacturing plants, workers develop their skills through informal on-the-job training, which focuses on casting, stonesetting, modelmaking, or engraving. To enter most technical programs, a high school diploma or an equivalent is required.

The precise and delicate nature of jewelry work requires finger and hand dexterity, good coordination, patience, and concentration. Artistic ability and fashion consciousness are major assets.

Income and Advancement

Depending on their employer, jewelers may receive commissions on what they sell or bonuses for outstanding work. Jewelers in retail stores earn a median salary of about $29,000 a year; jewelry repair workers earn a median salary of about $25,000 a year.

For those in manufacturing, earnings of experienced, unionized jewelry workers ranged from $10 to $12 an hour, according to limited information available.

Advancement opportunities are greatly dependent on an individual's skill and initiative. In manufacturing, jewelers can advance to supervisory jobs, such as master jeweler or head jeweler. Jewelers who work in jewelry stores or repair shops may become salaried managers. Some open their own businesses.

Where to Get More Information

Jewelers of America, 1185 Avenue of the Americas, New York, NY 10036.

Manufacturing Jewelers and Silversmiths of America, 100 India St., Providence, RI 02903.

Gemological Institute of America, 1660 Stewart St., Santa Monica, CA 90404.

Machinist

Job Description

Machinists are skilled workers who produce precision metal parts. These parts are used for the production and maintenance of industrial machinery, aircraft, automobiles, and many other manufactured goods. Machinists set up and operate a wide variety of machine tools and know the working properties of metals, such as steel, cast iron, aluminum, and brass. Using their skill with machine tools and their knowledge of metals, machinists plan and carry out the operations needed to make machine products that meet precise specifications.

Machinists first review blueprints or written specifications for a job. Then they calculate where to cut or bore into the workpiece, how fast to feed the metal into the machine, and how much metal to remove. They then select tools and materials for the job, plan the sequence of cutting and finishing operations, and mark the metal stock to show where these cuts should be made.

Then they position the metal stock on the machine tool, set the controls, and make the cuts. When machining operations are completed, they use precision instruments, such as micrometers, to make sure their work meets specifications. The next step is to finish and assemble the pieces.

Most machinists work in small machining shops or in manufacturing firms that produce durable goods, such as metalworking and industrial machinery, aircraft, or motor vehicles.

Qualifications

Machinist training varies from formal apprenticeship programs to informal on-the-job training. Most employers consider a formal apprenticeship program the best way to learn the trade. These programs consist of shop training and related classroom instructions.

Because machine shops have increased their use of computer-controlled equipment, training in the operation and programming of numerically controlled machine tools has become essential. Classroom instruction includes math, blueprint reading, mechanical drawing, and shop practices. Classroom training is increasingly being offered at community colleges in connection with company training programs.

Persons interested in becoming machinists should have manual dexterity and be mechanically inclined in order to use the tools and machines required to build complex parts. A high school or vocational school education, including mathematics, blueprint reading, metalworking, and drafting, is desirable.

Income and Advancement

Earnings of machinists compare favorably with those of other skilled workers. Median weekly earnings in 1993 were about $492 and ranged from $376 to $623, whereas the 10 percent with the highest earnings made more than $750 a week.

Where to Get More Information

The Association for Manufacturing Technology, 7901 Westpark Dr., McLean, VA 22102.

The National Tooling and Machining Association, 9300 Livingston Rd., Fort Washington, MD 20744.

The Tooling and Manufacturing Association, 1177 S. Dee Rd., Park Ridge, IL 60068.

Printing Press Operator

Job Description

Every newspaper, magazine, book, catalog, and piece of advertising literature that you see or read reflects the skills of printing press operators. They are responsible for the preparation, operation, and maintenance of printing presses of all sizes and capacities.

Printing press operators are generally classified according to the type of press they operate—offset, gravure, flexography, screen printing, or letterpress—and their duties vary accordingly.

Press preparation involves installing and adjusting the printing plate, adjusting pressure, inking presses, loading paper, and adjusting the press to paper size. Press operators must make sure that the paper and ink meet specifications, and they adjust control margins and the flow of ink to the inking roller accordingly. They then feed paper through the press cylinders and adjust feed and tension controls.

Press operators monitor the presses as they run, check their speed, correct uneven ink distribution, and adjust temperatures in the drying chamber. Operators oil and clean the presses and make minor repairs to keep them running smoothly. Those who work with large presses supervise assistants and helpers.

Press operators' jobs differ from one plant to another because of differences in kinds and sizes of presses. Small commercial shops generally have relatively small presses that print on one or two colors at a time and are operated by one person. Large newspaper, magazine, and book printers use giant "in-line web" presses that require a crew of several press operators and assistants. These presses are fed paper in big rolls, called "webs," up to 50 inches or more in width. Presses print the paper on both sides; trim, assemble, score, and fold the pages; and count the finished sections as they come off the press.

Modern plants use printing presses that incorporate computers and sophisticated instrumentation which controls press operations. With this equipment, press operators operate a control panel that monitors the printing process. To adjust the press, the operator pushes the appropriate button on the control panel.

Most jobs are in newspaper, magazine, and book printing plants or in firms that handle commercial or business printing. Commercial printing plants print newspaper inserts, catalogs, pamphlets, and the advertisements found in your mailbox. Additional jobs are in the "in-plant" department of organizations and corporations that do their own printing.

Qualifications

Entry-level workers generally start at the bottom and work their way up. With time, workers move up to operating one-color sheet-fed presses and may eventually advance to multicolor presses. Operators are likely to gain experience on many kinds of printing presses during the course of their career.

The apprenticeship period in commercial shops is four years for press operators. In addition to on-the-job instruction, the apprenticeship includes related classroom or correspondence school courses.

Press operators need good mechanical aptitude and an ability to visualize colors. Oral and writing skills also are required. Applicants should be able to compute percentages, weights, and measures; and they should possess enough mathematics skills to calculate the amount of ink and paper needed to do a job.

Income and Advancement

Salaries vary depending on the type of press being run and the area of the country in which the work is located. Median weekly earnings of press operators who work full time are about $430. The middle 50 percent earn between $310 and $575 a week, while the highest 10 percent earn more than $715 a week.

Press operators may advance in pay and responsibility by taking a job working on a more complex printing press. For example, a one-color sheet-fed press operator may, through experience and demonstrated ability, move to a four-color sheet-fed press. Others may be promoted to pressroom supervisor and be responsible for the work of an entire press crew.

Where to Get More Information

Graphic Communication International Union, 1900 L St., NW, Washington, DC 20036.

Graphic Arts Technical Foundaton, 4615 Forbes Ave., Pittsburgh, PA 15213.

Toolmaker and Diemaker

Job Description

Toolmakers craft precision tools that are used to cut, shape, and form metal and other materials. They also produce jigs and fixtures (devices that hold metal while it is bored, stamped, or drilled). Diemakers construct metal forms (dies) that are used to shape metal in stamping and forging operations. They also make metal molds for diecasting and for molding plastics, ceramics, and composite materials. Their craft requires finely honed skills enabling them to plan and build the precision equipment that is used in machines which produce a variety of products, from clothing and furniture to heavy equipment and aircraft parts.

Working from blueprints for instructions, toolmakers and diemakers plan the operations necessary to manufacture the tool or die. They then cut, bore, or drill the part, as required; assemble the parts; and perform finishing jobs such as filing, grinding, and polishing surfaces.

Toolmakers and diemakers work primarily in industries that manufacture metal-working machinery and equipment, motor vehicles, aircraft, and plastic products.

Qualifications

Most employers consider a formal apprenticeship program that combines classroom instruction and job experience the best way to learn all aspects of toolmaking and diemaking. A high school or vocational school education and, increasingly, an associate's degree, are preferred by most employers. Courses in math, blueprint reading, metalworking, and drafting, as well as machine shop experience, are helpful.

Apprentices learn to operate milling machines, lathes, grinders, and other machine tools. They also learn to use hand tools, gauges, and other mechanical equipment; and they study metal-working processes such as heat treating. Classroom training usually consists of mathematics, mechanical drawing, tool designing, tool programming, and blueprint reading.

Those who become toolmakers and diemakers without completing formal apprenticeships usually acquire their skills through on-the-job programs. They often begin as machine operators and are gradually given more difficult assignments.

Income and Advancement

Median weekly earnings for toolmakers and diemakers who worked full time were $642 in 1992. Most earned between $499 and $803 a week. Ten percent earned less than $409 a week, and the 10 percent with the highest weekly earnings made more than $911.

Skilled workers can move into supervisory and administrative positions in their firms; others become tool designers or tool programmers.

Where to Get More Information

The Association for Manufacturing Technology, 7901 Westpark Dr., McLean, VA 22102.

The National Tooling and Machining Association, 9300 Livingston Rd., Ft. Washington, MD 20744.

The Tooling and Manufacturing Association, 1177 S. Dee Rd., Park Ridge, IL 60068.

Precision Metalforming Association, 27027 Chardon Rd., Richmond Heights, OH 44143.

Welder, Cutter, and Welding Machine Operator

Job Description

Welding is the process of joining metal parts together by melting and fusing them to form a permanent bond. Because of its strength, welding is used to construct and repair parts of ships, automobiles, spacecraft, and thousands of other manufactured products. It is also used to join beams and steel reinforcing rods in building, bridges, and other structures.

Welders generally plan work by using drawings or specifications or by analyzing damaged metal, using their knowledge of welding and metals. Where the work is repetitive and the items to be welded relatively uniform, automatic welding is used. Here, a welding machine operator monitors the machine, which performs the welding tasks. Operators must constantly monitor the machine to ensure that it produces the desired weld.

The work of arc, plasma, and flame cutters is closely related to that of welders. Cutters use heat from burning gases or an electric arc to cut and trim rather than join metal.

Nearly seven out of ten welders work in plants that manufacture boilers, construction equipment, machinery, ships, motor vehicles, appliances, and other metal products. Most work in firms that construct bridges, buildings, pipelines, and other structures.

Qualifications

Training can range from a few days of school or on-the-job training for low-skilled positions, to several years of school and on-the-job training for highly skilled jobs. Formal training is available in high schools, vocational schools, technical institutes, and community colleges. Courses in blueprint reading, shop mathematics, mechanical drawing, physics, chemistry, and metallurgy are helpful.

Welders and cutters need manual dexterity, good eyesight, and good eye-hand coordination.

Income and Advancement

Median earnings for welders and welding machine operators are about $440 a week, and range from about $342 to more than $715. With additional training and experience, welders can advance to more skilled jobs. They may be promoted to welding technicians, supervisors, inspectors, or instructors. Some experienced welders open their own repair shops. More than one-third of welders belong to unions.

Where to Get More Information

Information on training opportunities and jobs can be obtained by contacting local employers and the local office of your state employment service.

Information on careers in welding is available from:

American Welding Society, 550 NW LeJeune Rd., P.O. Box 351040, Miami, FL 33135.

MECHANIC, INSTALLER, AND REPAIRER

••

Aircraft Mechanic

Job Description

Passenger and crew confidence in the safety and stability of the airplanes they fly in is a tribute to the skills of the mechanics and engine specialists who keep the airplanes in top condition.

The Federal Aviation Administration (FAA) sets precise schedules for the maintenance of all aircraft, based on the number of hours flown, days of operation, seasonal weather conditions, or a combination of these and other factors. All components of an aircraft, inside and out, are inspected regularly by mechanics. Engines, instruments, landing gear, pressurized systems, pumps, valves, brakes, air conditioners, and heaters are only a few of the many parts that are systematically examined and tested for reliability according to strict engineering standards.

Engines are periodically stripped down by engine specialists who use precision instruments and state-of-the-art electronic and magnetic test equipment to check every system to ensure that it will operate safely and efficiently under all possible conditions. Outside surfaces of the aircraft are checked for invisible cracks or signs of corrosion, wear, and metal fatigue. Mechanics then make necessary repairs and install replacement parts.

Qualifications

The majority of mechanics who work on civilian aircraft are certificated by the FAA in the area in which they are specialized. The FAA requires at least 18 months of work experience for an airframe, powerplant, or repairman's certificate, and 30 months of experience working with both airframes and engines. Applicants for certificates must pass written and oral tests and demonstrate they can do the work authorized by the certificate.

Most mechanics learn their job in the military or in one of about 150 trade schools certified by the FAA. A few learn through on-the-job training. Trade-school courses run from two years to 30 months and provide training with tools and equipment used on the job. Courses in mathematics, physics, chemistry, electronics, computers, or mechanical drawing are helpful. Mechanical aptitude is necessary, as is the ability to diagnose and solve complex mechanical problems. Many mechanics take courses offered by manufacturers or employers, usually through outside contractors.

Experienced aircraft mechanics have opportunities for higher levels of responsibility, such as crew chief, lead inspector, and shop supervisor. In commercial airlines, where promotion is determined by examination, supervisors may advance to executive positions.

Income and Advancement

Salaries range from $30,000 to $40,000 per year, with the top 10 percent earning more than $46,500. Commercial mechanics who work on jets generally earn more than those who work on other aircraft. Commercial airline mechanics generally earn more than mechanics working for other employers. Many mechanics, including those employed by some major airlines, are covered by union agreements where salaries and benefits are set by labor contracts.

Where to Get More Information

Information about jobs with a particular airline may be obtained by writing to the personnel manager of the company. For addresses of airlines and information about opportunities, contact:

Future Aviation Professionals of America, 4959 Massachusetts Blvd., Atlanta, GA 30337. Or call 1-800-JET-JOBS.

Aviation Maintenance Foundation, P.O. Box 2826, Redmond, WA 98073.

Professional Aviation Maintenance Association, 500 Northwest Plaza, Suite 401, St. Ann, MO 63074.

Automotive Body Repairer

Job Description

Traffic accidents are a daily occurrence in every city, town, and hamlet in America. The resulting damage to cars and other motor vehicles keeps many thousands of car repairers busy removing dents, straightening bent bodies, and replacing crumbled parts that are beyond repair. Most repairers work on cars and small trucks; some work on large trucks, buses, or tractor trailers.

Automotive body repairers use special machines to restore damaged metal frames and body sections to their original shape and location. They remove badly damaged sections of body panels with a pneumatic metal-cutting gun or acetylene torch and weld in new sections to replace them. Repairers pull out less serious dents with a hydraulic jack or hand prying bar, or knock them out with hand tools or pneumatic hammers. They smooth out small dents and creases in the metal, and remove every small pit and dimple with pick hammers and punches.

Body repairers also repair or replace the plastic body parts used increasingly on newer-model vehicles. They remove the damaged panels, and, after determining the type of plastic from which they are made, they can apply heat from a hot-air welding gun or immerse them in hot water so that they can press the softened panels back into their original shape by hand. They replace plastic parts that are more difficult to repair.

In large shops, body repairers may specialize in one type of repair, such as frame straightening or door and fender repairing. Some also specialize in installing glass.

Most body repairers work for shops that specialize in body repairs or painting, and for automobile and truck dealers. Others work for organizations that maintain their own motor vehicles, such as trucking companies and automobile rental companies. A few work for motor vehicle manufacturers. About one in five is self-employed.

Qualifications

Many repairers enter the occupation by transferring from related helper positions. Those who know how to use hand tools learn the trade as helpers, picking up skills on the job.

Most employers prefer to hire persons who have completed formal training programs in automotive body repair. Formal training is highly desirable because advances in technology in recent years have greatly changed the structure, components, and materials used in automobiles. As a result, many new repair problems have been created and many new skills are required.

Automotive body-repair training programs are offered in high schools, vocational schools, private trade schools, and community colleges.

Employers hire many trainees without formal automotive body-repair training, but most prefer to hire high school graduates. Because workers must constantly refer to technical manuals and make very precise measurements, good reading and basic mathematics skills are essential.

Repairers must buy their own hand tools, but employers usually furnish power tools. Trainees generally accumulate tools as they gain experience, and many workers have thousands of dollars invested in tools.

Income and Advancement

Body repairers average weekly earnings of about $289 to $525, with the highest 10 percent earning more than $757. The majority employed by dealers and repair shops are paid on an incentive basis. With this method, they are paid a predetermined amount for various tasks, and earnings depend on the amount of work assigned and how fast it is completed. Repairers are frequently guaranteed a minimum weekly salary.

An experienced automotive body repairer with supervisory ability may advance to shop supervisor or service manager. Some open their own body-repair shops, and others become automobile damage appraisers for insurance companies.

Where to Get More Information

Automotive Service Industry Association, 25 Northwest Point, Elk Grove, IL 60007.

National Automotive Technician Education Foundation, 13505 Dulles Technology Dr., Herndon, VA 22071.

For information on local training facilities and jobs, contact the local office of your state employment service.

Automotive Mechanic

Job Description

Anyone whose car has broken down appreciates the skills of the automobile mechanic. The ability to diagnose the source of a problem quickly and accurately is one of the mechanic's most important skills.

Automobile mechanics or automotive service technicians repair and service automobiles, light trucks, and other gasoline-powered vehicles, such as pickups and vans. Those who receive specialized training and experience can become diesel mechanics qualified to repair and service diesel-powered trucks, buses, and other diesel-powered equipment. Others learn how to handle motorcycles, motorscooters, and specialized all-terrain vehicles.

Mechanics perform routine service, inspecting, lubricating, and adjusting engines and other equipment. They repair or replace worn parts, such as hoses, belts, spark plugs, and bearings, and attend to other potential trouble spots to keep the car running smoothly and efficiently.

Modern automobiles are precision machines requiring the use of specialized precision tools. Factory-installed computers monitor engine performance, fuel control, and brake systems. No longer are the screwdriver, monkey wrench, and grease gun the mechanic's main tools. Mechanics now use such power tools as pneumatic wrenches to remove bolts quickly, grinding machines to rebuild brakes and other parts, welding and cutting equipment to remove and repair exhaust systems, and power jacks and hoists to lift cars and engines. State-of-the-art electronic systems, such as infrared analyzers and computerized diagnostic devices, detect trouble spots with unerring accuracy, enabling the mechanic to pinpoint problems quickly and make the necessary adjustments.

In an age of specialization, automobile mechanics are no exception. For instance, automatic transmission mechanics work on gear trains, hydraulic pumps, couplings, and other parts of the transmission system. Tune-up specialists adjust ignition timing and valves. Using electronic equipment, they identify malfunctions and adjust and replace spark plugs, fuel, and ignition systems. Air-conditioning specialists repair and service compressors and condensors. Front-end mechanics align and balance wheels, steering, and suspension systems. Brake specialists adjust brakes, replace linings, repair hydraulic cylinders, and make other repairs on brake systems.

The majority of mechanics work for automotive dealers, independent repair shops, or gasoline service stations. Some are employed by department, automotive, or home supply stores. Others are employed by taxi fleets; automobile leasing companies; and federal, state, or local government agencies. Automobile manufacturers maintain a staff of mechanics at their plants to adjust cars at the end of assembly lines. About 20 percent of mechanics are self-employed.

Qualifications

The modern car is a far cry from the relatively simple machine of yesteryear when a mechanic needed little more than a set of screwdrivers and wrenches to make repairs. Although some automotive mechanics still learn the trade solely by assisting and working with experienced mechanics, the rapidly increasing technology requires formal training after graduation from high school. Electronics is being used in a variety of automotive components. Engine controls and dashboard instruments were among the first to use electronics, but now it is being used in brakes, transmissions, and steering systems. Each new model year brings new applications of electronically operated systems. This means that most automotive mechanics must be familiar with at least the basic principles of electronics to function efficiently.

Courses in automotive repairs and maintenance are offered in high schools, community colleges, and public and private vocational and technical schools. High school programs, while an asset, vary greatly in quality. Some offer only an introduction to automotive technology for the car owner or hobbyist, whereas others aim to equip graduates with enough skills to get a job as a trainee mechanic.

Training programs vary greatly, but they generally provide a combination of classroom instruction and hands-on practice. Some trade school programs concentrate the instruction in six months to a year. Community colleges spread the program over two years, supplementing the instruction in English, basic mathematics, and other subjects leading to an associate degree.

Automobile manufacturers and dealers sponsor two-year programs at about 90 community colleges across the nation. They provide late-model cars, tools, and equipment on which the students practice. Students then spend alternate six- to twelve-week periods attending classes full time and working full time in the service departments of dealers. Some sponsors provide financial assistance where needed.

Trainee mechanics need good reading and basic mathematics skills in order to read and understand technical manuals to keep up with new technology. They also must possess mechanical aptitude and a knowledge of how automobiles work. Most employers require completion of a vocational training program in automotive mechanics. Experience gained in the Armed Forces or as a hobby is also valuable. A high school diploma or equivalency is also required by most employers.

Beginners entering on-the-job training programs start as mechanics' helpers and are required to serve as lubrication workers and gasoline service station attendants. It takes anywhere from one to two years to acquire proficiency to become a journeyman mechanic. Graduates of trade schools or community colleges are often able to earn promotion to journeyman after only a few months on the job. An additional year or two of experience is required to become thoroughly familiar with all types of repairs.

Many employers send experienced automotive mechanics to factory training centers to learn to repair new models or to receive special training. Dealers may also send promising beginners to factory-sponsored training programs. In addition, factory representatives come to many shops to conduct short training sessions.

Income and Advancement

Median weekly earnings of automotive mechanics who are wage and salary workers were $408 in 1992. The middle 50 percent earned between $320 and $523 a week, while the top 10 percent earned more than $746 a week. Many mechanics employed by dealers and independent repair shops receive a commission related to the labor cost charged to the customer. Under this method, weekly earnings can vary considerably depending on the amount of work the mechanic does. Employers frequently guarantee commissioned mechanics a minimum weekly salary. Some mechanics belong to labor unions that have contracts with employers establishing pay rates, hours, and working conditions. Most mechanics can expect steady work because changes in the economy seem to have little effect on the automotive repair business.

Experienced mechanics with leadership skills can advance to the position of service manager. Those who work well with customers can become repair service estimators. Many experienced mechanics open independent repair shops.

Where to Get More Information

National Automotive Technicians Education Foundation, 13505 Dulles Technology Dr., Herndon, VA 22071.

Training Development, Ford Parts and Service Division, Ford Motor Company, 3000 Schaefer Rd., Dearborn, MI 48121.

Chrysler Dealer Apprenticeship Program, National C.A.P. Coordinator, 26001 Lawrence Ave., Center Line, MI 48015.

General Motors Automotive Service Educational Program, National College Coordinator, General Motors Technical Service, 30501 Van Dyke Ave., Warren, MI 48090.

Automotive Service Association, Inc., P.O. Box 929, Bedford, TX 76095.

Automotive Service Industry Association, 25 Northwest Point, Elk Village, IL 60007.

Computer and Office Machine Service Technician

Job Description

"The computer is down" is a statement heard often in the electronic age. Keeping computers and other office machinery at maximum efficiency is the job of computer and office machine service technicians. They install new machines, do preventive maintenance, and correct emergency problems.

Computer service technicians work on all types of computer equipment and word processing systems, whereas office machine technicians work on photocopiers, cash registers, fax machines, and other similar equipment. They may make special cable and wiring connections when installing equipment. Service technicians work closely with electricians, who install the wiring for new systems, to ensure proper layout.

Despite frequent preventive maintenance, computers do break down. To locate the cause of failures, service technicians run diagnostic programs that pinpoint malfunctions. Although some of the most modern and sophisticated computers have a self-diagnosing capacity that directs technicians to the source of the problem, computer repairers must know enough about systems software to determine whether the malfunction is due to an error in the hardware or software.

Qualifications

Computer and office machine service technicians should be high school graduates. Courses in electricity or electronics are helpful. Employers also look for education in trade or technical school or a two-year community college. Service technicians should have good hand dexterity and be able to read an electrical diagram or schematic.

Some service company employers train beginners in the repair and maintenance of the equipment they sell or lease, and many manufacturers also offer training courses through workers' employers.

Income and Advancement

Median annual earnings of full-time computer and office machine service technicians are about $25,200. Earnings vary widely depending on the type of equipment involved and the size and geographical location of the company.

Where to Get More Information

The International Society of Certified Electronics Technicians, 2708 W. Berry St., Fort Worth, TX 76109.

Electronics Association, 604 N. Jackson, Greencastle, IN 46135.

Diesel Mechanic

Job Description

The average driver whose automobile runs on gasoline gives little thought to the diesel engine. Yet the diesel engine powers most of America's heavy trucks, buses, and locomotives. Diesels are also used to run bulldozers, cranes, road graders, tractors, and combines, plus a variety of other equipment, such as electric generators, compressors, and pumps used in oil-well digging and in irrigation. Diesel engines are also installed in a small number of automobiles.

The diesel engine is more durable and usually heavier than gasoline engines, but diesels use fuel more efficiently because they convert a higher percentage of fuel into power.

Diesel mechanics repair and maintain diesel engines of all sizes for all types of equipment. Those who work for organizations that maintain their own vehicles may spend much time doing preventive maintenance to ensure safe operation, prevent wear and damage to parts, and reduce costly breakdowns. In many shops, mechanics do all kinds of repairs, working on a vehicle's electrical system one day and doing major engine repairs the next. They use a variety of tools, such as pneumatic wrenches and welding and flame-cutting equipment, in addition to common hand tools.

Nearly one-third of diesel mechanics service trucks and other diesel-powered equipment for customers of vehicle and equipment dealers, leasing companies, and independent automotive repair shops. Over one-fifth work for local and long-distance trucking companies, and over one-fifth maintain the buses and trucks of buslines, public transit companies, school systems, and federal, state, and local governments. The remainder maintain the fleets of trucks and other equipment of manufacturing, construction, and other companies. A relatively small number are self-employed.

Qualifications

Most employers prefer to hire graduates of formal postsecondary training programs in diesel mechanics, but many mechanics still learn their skills on the job. Beginners, especially those having automobile service experience, start as mechanics' helpers. They advance to increasingly difficult jobs as they prove their ability. After they master the repair and service of diesel engines, they learn to work on other components such as brakes, transmissions, or electrical systems.

For unskilled entry-level jobs, employers generally look for applicants who have mechanical aptitude and are at least 18 years of age and in good physical condition. Completion of high school is required by a growing number of employers. Courses in automotive repair, electronics, English, mathematics, and physics provide a good basic educational background for a career as a diesel mechanic. A state chauffeur's license is needed for test driving trucks or buses on public roads.

Income and Advancement

Earnings of diesel mechanics average from $14.60 to $17.10 an hour, depending on the industry and geographical location.

Opportunities should be good for persons who complete formal training in diesel mechanics at community and junior colleges and vocational and technical schools. Experienced mechanics who have leadership ability may advance to shop supervisor or service manager positions. Mechanics who have sales ability sometimes become sales representatives. Some open their own repair shops.

Electronic Equipment Service Technician

Job Description

Electronic service technicians, also called electronic equipment repairers or field service representatives, install, maintain, and repair electronic equipment used in offices, factories, homes, hospitals, aircraft, and other places. This equipment includes televisions, radar, industrial equipment controls, computers, telephone systems, and medical diagnosing equipment.

Electronic repairers install, test, repair, and calibrate equipment to ensure that it functions properly. They use voltmeters, ohmmeters, signal generators, ammeters, and oscilloscopes and run diagnostic programs to pinpoint malfunctions. To fix equipment, repairers may replace defective components, circuit boards, or wiring, or adjust and calibrate equipment, using small hand tools.

Field repairers visit worksites to do preventive maintenance according to manufacturers' recommended schedules—and whenever emergencies arise.

Bench repairers work at repair facilities or in stores, factories, or service centers. They repair portable equipment, such as televisions and personal computers, brought in by customers, or defective components and machines requiring extensive repairs that have been sent in by field repairers.

Qualifications

Applicants for entry-level positions must have some training in electronics, acquired formally on the job. Formal training is offered by public postsecondary vocational-technical schools, private vocational schools and technical institutes, junior and community colleges, and some high schools and correspondence schools.

Training includes general courses in mathematics, physics, electricity, electronics, schematic reading, and troubleshooting. Students may choose courses to prepare them for a specialty, such as computers, commercial and industrial equipment, or home entertainment equipment. Those who want to specialize in testing and repairing radio transmitting equipment, other than business and and mobile radios, need a General Operators License from the Federal Communications Commission.

Income and Advancement

Median weekly earnings in 1992 for full-time electronic equipment repairers were about $521. The middle 50 percent earned between $406 and $629, while the top 10 percent earned more than $729. Earnings will vary by occupation and the type of equipment repaired.

Experienced repairers with advanced training may become specialists or troubleshooters who help other repairers diagnose difficult problems, or who work with engineers in designing equipment and developing maintenance procedures. Because of their familiarity with equipment, repairers are particularly well-qualified to become manufacturers' sales representatives. Those with leadership ability also may become maintenance supervisors or service managers. Some experienced workers open their own repair services or shops, or become wholesalers or retailers of electronic equipment.

Where to Get More Information

The International Society of Certified Electronics Technicians, 2708 W. Berry St., Fort Worth, TX 76109.

Electronics Technicians Association, 604 N. Jackson, Greencastle, IN 46135.

Federal Communications Commission, 1919 M St., NW, Washington, DC 20554.

Heating, Air-Conditioning, and Refrigeration Technician

Job Description

People always have sought ways to make their environment more comfortable. Today, heating and air-conditioning systems control the temperature, humidity, and air quality in residential, commercial, industrial, and other buildings. Refrigeration makes it possible to store and transport food, medicine, and other perishable items. Heating, air-conditioning, and refrigeration technicians install, maintain, and repair these systems.

Heating equipment technicians follow blueprints or other specifications to install oil, gas, electricity, solid fuel, and multifuel heating systems; and, after installation, they perform routine maintenance and repairs in order to keep the system operating efficiently.

Air-conditioning and refrigeration technicians install and service central air-conditioning systems and a variety of refrigeration equipment. They follow blueprints, design specifications, and manufacturers' instructions to install motors, compressors, condensing units, evaporators, and other components.

Heating, air-conditioning, and refrigeration technicians work in homes, supermarkets, hospitals, office buildings, factories—anywhere there is climate control equipment. About half work for cooling and heating contractors. The remainder are employed in a wide variety of industries. Some work for fuel oil dealers, utilities companies, and refrigeration and air-conditioning repair shops. Others are employed by hospitals, office buildings, and other organizations that operate large climate control systems. Approximately one of every seven is self-employed.

Qualifications

Employers prefer to hire technicians with technical school or apprenticeship training. A large number of these workers, however, still learn the trade informally on the job. Many technical trade schools and junior and community colleges offer programs in theory, design, and equipment construction, as well as electronics.

Courses in shop math, mechanical drawing, applied physics and chemistry, electronics, and blueprint reading provide a good background for those interested in entering this occupation. A basic understanding of microelectronics is becoming more important because of the increasing use of solid-state equipment controls.

Income and Advancement

Median weekly earnings of air-conditioning, heating, and refrigeration technicians on salary are $474. The middle 50 percent earn between $356 and $596, and the top 10 percent earn more than $743 a week.

Advancement usually takes the form of higher wages. Some technicians advance to positions as supervisors. Those with sufficient money and managerial skill can open their own contracting businesses.

Where to Get More Information

Associated Builders and Contractors, 1300 N. 17th St., Rosslyn, VA 22209.

Refrigeration Service Engineers Society, 1666 Rand Rd., Des Plaines, IL 60016.

National Association of Home Builders, Home Builders Institute, 1010 Vermont Ave., NW, Washington, DC 20005.

National Association of Plumbing, Heating, and Cooling Contractors, P.O. Box 6808, Falls Church, VA 22040.

Air Conditioning and Refrigeration Institute, 1501 Wilson Blvd., Arlington, VA 22209.

Millwright

Job Description

Millwrights install, repair, replace, and dismantle the machinery and heavy equipment used in almost every industry. Known as jacks-of-all-trades, millwrights have responsibilities that require a wide range of skills—from blueprint reading and pouring concrete to diagnosing and solving mechanical problems.

When machinery arrives at the job sight, millwrights unload, inspect, and move the equipment into position. Because they often have to decide what device to use for moving machinery, they must know the load-bearing properties of ropes, cables, hoists, and cranes.

New machinery sometimes requires a new foundation. Millwrights prepare the foundation or supervise its construction. They must know how to read blueprints and work with building materials, such as concrete, wood, and steel.

When assembling machinery, millwrights fit bearings, align gears and wheels, attach motors, and connect belts according to the manufacturer's specifications and drawings. They must have good mathematical skills so that they can measure angles, material thickness, and small distances with tools such as squares, calipers, and micrometers. They also use hand and power tools, cutting torches, and soldering guns. Some use metalworking equipment, such as lathes or grinders, to modify parts to specifications.

Millwrights are employed in either manufacturing or construction. Over 70 percent work in the durable-goods manufacturing industries, such as basic steel products and motor vehicles and equipment. Most of the rest are employed by construction firms and companies providing millwright services on a contract basis.

Qualifications

Millwrights receive their training from a formal apprenticeship program or informally on the job. Apprenticeship programs usually combine four years of on-the-job training with classroom instruction in mathematics, blueprint reading, hydraulics, electricity, and computers. Strength and agility are important, as are good interpersonal and communication abilities in order to work as part of a team and give detailed instructions to others.

Income and Advancement

Median weekly earnings of full-time millwrights are about $598. The middle 50 percent earn between $479 and $724, while the top 10 percent earn more than $840. Earnings vary by industry and geographic locations. Many millwrights belong to labor unions.

Where to Get More Information

Associated General Contractors of America, 1957 E St., NW, Washington, DC 20006.

For further information on apprenticeship programs, write to the Apprenticeship Council of your state's labor department or to local offices of your state employment service.

Line Installer and Cable Splicer

Job Description

Transmitting the electric power produced in generating plants to individual customers, connecting telephone central offices to customers' telephone and switchboards, and extending cable TV to residential and commercial customers requires a vast network of wires and cables. To connect and maintain this network requires the skills and know-how of line installers and cable splicers.

To install new electric power or telephone lines, line installers or line erectors install poles and terminals, erect towers, and place wires and cable. They climb poles or use truck-mounted buckets and use handtools to attach the cables. When working with electric power lines, they may install transformers, circuit breakers, switches, or other equipment. To bury underground cable, they use trenchers, plows, and other power equipment.

Line installers also lay cable television lines underground or hang them on poles with telephone and utility wires. These lines transmit broadcast signals from microwave towers to customers' homes. They also place wiring in the home, connect the customers' television sets to it, and check that the television signal is strong.

After telephone line installers lay cables in place, cable splicing technicians complete the line connections. They connect individual wires or fibers within the cable and rearrange wires when lines have to be changed.

Line installers and cable splicers usually work outdoors and are subject to 24-hour call. Most usually work a 40-hour week, but when severe weather damages transmission and distribution lines, they may work long and irregular hours to restore service. At times, they may travel to distant locations, and occasionally they stay for a lengthy period to help restore damaged facilities or build new ones.

Qualifications

Most employers prefer high school graduates. Many test applicants for basic verbal, arithmetic, and reasoning skills. Some test for physical ability, such as balance, coordination, and mechanical aptitude.

Line installers and cable splicers in electric companies and construction firms generally complete a formal apprenticeship program. Workers in telephone companies generally receive several years of informal on-the-job training. They may also attend training provided by equipment manufacturers.

Formal training includes instruction in electrical codes, blueprint reading, and basic electrical theory.

Income and Advancement

Pay rates for line installers and cable splicers vary greatly across the country and depend on length of service. In 1992, line installers and repairers who worked full time earned a median weekly wage of $648. The middle 50 percent earned between $503 and $770, with the top 10 percent earning more than $874 a week.

Most line installers and cable splicers belong to unions, principally the Communications Workers of America and the International Brotherhood of Electrical Workers. Union contracts set wage rates, wage increases, and the time needed to advance from one step to the next. These contracts require extra pay for overtime and for all work on Sundays and holidays. Most contracts provide for additional pay for night work.

For installers in the telephone industry, advancement may come about through promotion to splicer. Splicers can advance to engineering assistants or may move into other kinds of work, such as sales. Promotion to a supervisory position also is possible.

Where to Get More Information

For more details about employment opportunities, contact the telephone or electric power company in your community or local offices of the unions that represent these workers. For general information on line installer and cable splicer jobs, contact:

Communications Workers of America, 501 3rd St., NW, Washington, DC 20001.

For additional information on the telephone industry and careers opportunities, contact:

United States Telephone Association, Small Companies Division, 900 19th St., NW, Washington, DC 20006.

PROTECTIVE SERVICES

● ●

Correction Officer

Job Description

The safety and security of persons who have been arrested, are awaiting trial, or have been convicted of a crime and sentenced to serve time in a correction institution are the responsibility of the nation's correction officers.

They escort prisoners in transit between courtrooms, correction institutions, and other points. They maintain order within the institution; enforce rules and regulations; and often supplement the counseling that inmates receive from psychologists, social workers, and other mental health professionals.

Correction officers monitor inmates' activities, including working, exercising, and eating. They also supervise inmates' work assignments as well as instruct and help them on specific tasks. It is sometimes necessary to settle disputes and to enforce discipline. To prevent escapes, officers staff security positions in towers and at gates.

Correction officers report orally and in writing on inmate conduct and on the quality and quantity of work done. They report disturbances, violations of rules, and any unusual occurrences.

Counseling and helping inmates with problems are increasingly important parts of the correction officer's job. Institutions usually employ psychologists and social workers to counsel inmates, but corrections officers informally supplement the work of the professionals. In some institutions, officers receive specialized training in counseling.

About three-fifths of corrections officers work at state correctional institutions, such as prisons, prison camps, and reformatories. Most of the remainder work at city and county jails or other institutions run by local governments. A few thousand work at federal correctional institutions.

Qualifications

Most institutions require that correction officers must meet an 18- or 21-year age minimum, have a high school education or equivalent, and be a U.S. citizen. In addition, institutions increasingly seek correction officers with some additional education in psychology and criminology, reflecting a continuing emphasis on personal counseling and rehabilitation. Correction officers must be in good health, physically fit, have good judgment, and have the ability to think and act quickly.

The federal government, as well as almost every state and a few localities, provides training for correction officers. All states and local departments of correction provide informal on-the-job training. Academy trainees generally receive several weeks or months of instruction about institutional policies, regulations, and operations; counseling psychology; crises intervention; inmate behavior, rules, and rights; contraband control; administrative responsibilities; self-defense; the use of firearms; and physical fitness training. Officers employed by the federal government and most state governments are covered by civil service systems or merit boards. In 36 out of the 50 states in the United States, correction officers are represented by labor unions.

Income and Advancement

Starting salaries of state correction officers averaged about $18,600 a year in 1992, depending on the location of the facility. Salaries generally were comparable for correction officers working in jails and other county and municipal correctional institutions. At the federal level, the starting salary was about $18,300 a year in 1993; supervisory correction officers started at about $40,300 a year. The 1993 average salary for all federal nonsupervisory correction officers was about $30,000; for supervisors, about $53,000.

With additional education, experience, or training, qualified officers may advance to other supervisory, administrative, or counseling positions. Officers sometimes transfer to related areas, such as probation and parole.

Where to Get More Information

Information about entrance requirements, training, and career opportunities may be obtained from the Federal Office of Personnel Management, Federal Bureau of Prisons, state civil service commissions, state departments of correction, or local correctional institutions and facilities.

Additional information on careers in corrections is available from:

The American Correctional Association, 8025 Laurel Lakes Ct., Laurel, MD 20707.

American Probation and Parole Association, P.O. Box 201, Salt Lake City, UT 84152.

The International Association of Correctional Officers, 1133 S. Wabash Ave., Chicago, IL 60605.

Firefighter

Job Description

Each year fire kills thousands of people and destroys billions of dollars worth of property. Career firefighters help protect the public against this hazard.

Firefighting requires a high degree of organization and teamwork. At every fire, firefighters perform specific duties assigned by an officer, such as connecting hose lines to hydrants, operating pumps, or positioning ladders. They rescue victims and administer emergency medical aid, ventilate smoke-filled areas, operate equipment, and salvage the contents of buildings.

Due to the use of increasingly sophisticated equipment, the job of firefighter has become more complex. Many firefighters have additional responsibilities—for example, working with ambulance services that provide emergency medical treatment; assisting in the recovery from natural disasters, such as earthquakes, floods, and tornadoes; and becoming involved with the control and cleanup of oil spills and other hazardous chemical incidents.

Most fire departments also are responsible for fire prevention. Specially trained personnel inspect public buildings for conditions that might cause a fire, such as fire escapes and fire doors, the storage of flammable materials, and other possible hazards. In addition, firefighters educate the public about fire prevention and safety measures. They frequently speak on this subject before school assemblies and civic groups.

Firefighters spend much of their time at fire stations, which usually have facilities for dining and sleeping. They also receive training, clean and maintain equipment, conduct practice drills, and participate in physical fitness activities.

More than nine out of 10 firefighters work in municipal fire departments. Some work in fire departments of federal and state installations, including airports. Relatively few are employed by private firefighting companies.

Qualifications

Applicants for municipal firefighting jobs may have to pass a written examination; tests of strength, stamina, and agility; and a medical evaluation. Examinations are open to applicants who are at least 18 years of age and have a high school education or the equivalent.

As a rule, beginners in large fire departments are trained for several weeks at the department's training center. They study firefighting techniques, fire prevention, hazardous materials, local building codes, and emergency medical procedures. A growing number of fire departments have accredited apprenticeship programs, which combine formal, technical instruction with on-the-job training under the supervision of experienced firefighters.

Many colleges offer courses leading to two-year degrees in fire engineering or fire science, and a few offer four-year degrees. Most fire captains and other supervisory personnel have some college training.

Income and Advancement

Earnings vary considerably depending on city size and region of the country. Average annual earnings range from about $26,200 in the smallest cities to $42,848 in the largest. The top 10 percent earn about $51,324. Higher-ranking officers earn more. The majority of career firefighters are members of the International Association of Fire Fighters, which negotiates salaries and benefits.

To progress to higher-level positions, firefighters must acquire expertise in the most advanced firefighting equipment and techniques, management and budgeting procedures, emergency medical procedures, and labor relations. Some attend training sessions sponsored by the National Fire Academy on such topics as executive development, anti-arson techniques, and public fire safety and education. As firefighters gain experience, they may advance to a higher rank. They may become eligible for promotion to the grade of lieutenant. The line of further promotion usually is to captain, then battalion chief, assistant chief, deputy chief, and chief. Advancement generally depends upon scores on written examination, performance on the job, and seniority.

Where to Get More Information

Information on obtaining a job as a firefighter is available from local civil service offices or fire departments and from the following organization:

International Association of Fire Fighters, 1750 New York Ave., NW, Washington, DC 20036.

Additional information on the salaries and hours of work in various cities is published annually by the International City Management Association in its *Municipal Yearbook*, which is available in many libraries.

Police Officer, Detective, and Special Agent

Job Description

Police officers, detectives, and special agents are responsible for the safety of America's cities, towns, and highways. Police officers and detectives who work in small communities and rural areas have diversified duties. They may direct traffic at the scene of a fire or an accident, investigate a burglary, or give first aid to an accident or crime victim.

By comparison, in a large urban police department, officers are usually assigned to a specific type of duty. Most are detailed to patrol or to traffic duty. Some are experts in chemical and microscopic analysis, firearms identification, or handwriting and fingerprint identification. Some are assigned to special units, such as mounted and motorcycle police, harbor and helicopter patrols, mobile rescue teams, and youth aid services.

Sheriffs and deputy sheriffs generally enforce the law in rural areas where there may not be a police department. Bailiffs are responsible for keeping order in courtrooms. U.S. marshals serve civil writs and criminal warrants issued by federal judges. Detectives and special agents are plainclothes investigators who gather facts and collect evidence for criminal cases.

Federal Bureau of Investigation (FBI) special agents investigate violations of federal laws. Agents with specialized training usually work on cases related to their background. For example, agents with an accounting background may investigate white-collar crimes, such as bank embezzlements or fraudulent bankruptcies.

Special agents employed by the U.S. Department of Treasury work for the U.S. Customs Service; the Bureau of Alcohol, Tobacco, and Firearms; the U.S. Secret Service; and the Internal Revenue Service. Custom agents enforce laws to prevent smuggling of goods across U.S. borders. Alcohol, Tobacco, and Firearms agents might investigate suspected illegal sales of guns or underpayment of federal sales taxes. U.S. Secret Service agents protect the president and vice-president and their immediate families, presidential candidates, ex-presidents, and foreign dignitaries visiting the United States. They also investigate counterfeiting, forgery of government checks or bonds, and the fraudulent use of credit cards. Special agents of the Internal Revenue Service collect evidence against individuals and firms that are evading payment of federal taxes.

Federal drug enforcement agents conduct criminal investigations of illicit drug activity.

State police officers, also known as state troopers or highway patrol officers, patrol highways and enforce traffic regulations. State police officers sometimes check the weight of commercial vehicles, conduct driver examinations, and give information on highway safety to the public. In most states, they also enforce criminal laws in communities and counties that do not have a local police force or in large sheriffs' departments.

Qualifications

The appointment of police and detectives in practically all jurisdictions is governed by civil service regulations. Candidates must be U.S. citizens, usually at least 20 years of age, and must meet rigorous physical and personal qualifications.

In large police departments, where most jobs are found, applicants usually must have a high school education. A number of cities and states require some college training. Some specialized departments within the police establishment may require a college degree. In a few cases, a police department will accept recruits who do not have a high school diploma, particularly if they have worked in a field related to law enforcement.

Educational requirements for applicants for federal agent positions vary. Although many positions require a college degree, law enforcement experience in combination with special training may be acceptable. For an appointment as an FBI special agent, however, an applicant must be a graduate of an accredited law school; be a college graduate with a major in accounting, engineering, or computer science; or be a college graduate with either fluency in a foreign language or three years of full-time work experience. Applicants must be U.S. citizens, between 23 and 35 years of age, and willing to accept assignment anywhere in the country. All new agents undergo 15 weeks of training at the FBI Academy on the U.S. Marine Corps base in Quantico, Virginia.

Applicants for special agent jobs with the U.S. Department of Treasury must have a bachelor's degree or a minimum of three years' work experience of which at least two are in criminal investigation. Treasury agents undergo eight weeks of training at the Federal Law Enforcement Training Center in Glynco, Georgia, and another eight weeks of specialized training with their particular bureau.

Income and Advancement

Average salaries in 1992 for police officers and detectives were about $32,000 a year. The middle 50 percent earned between about $25,000 and $41,200, while the highest-paid 10 percent earned over $51,200 a year. Salaries tend to be higher in larger urban jurisdictions with bigger police departments.

Police officers and detectives in supervisory positions average about $38,100 a year. The middle 50 percent earn between about $28,200 and $49,800; the highest-paid 10 percent, more than $58,400 annually.

Officers usually become eligible for promotion after a probationary period ranging from six months to three years. In large departments, promotion may enable an officer to become a detective or specialize in one type of work, such as laboratory analysis of evidence, traffic control, communications, or work with juveniles. Promotions to sergeant, lieutenant, and captain usually are made according to a candidate's position on a promotion list, as determined by the results of a written examination and on-the-job performance.

In 1993, FBI agents started at about $30,600 a year, while Treasury Department agents started at about $18,700 to $22,700 a year. Salaries of experienced FBI agents started at approximately $47,900, while supervisory agents started at around $56,600 a year.

Total earnings frequently exceed the stated salary due to payments for overtime, which can be significant, especially during criminal investigations when police are needed for crowd control during sporting events or political rallies. In addition to common fringe benefits—paid vacation, sick leave, and medical and life insurance—most police departments and federal agencies provide officers with special allowances for uniforms and furnish revolvers, handcuffs, and other required equipment. Because they are generally covered by liberal pension plans, many retire at half-pay after 20 or 25 years of service.

Where to Get More Information

Information about entrance requirements may be obtained from federal, state, and local civil service commissions or police departments. Contact any office of Personnel Management Job Information Center for pamphlets providing general information and instructions for submitting an application for jobs as Treasury special agents, drug enforcement agents, FBI special agents, or U.S. marshals. Look under U.S. Government, Office of Personnel Management, in your local telephone directory to obtain a telephone number.

Information about law enforcement careers in general may be obtained from:

International Union of Police Associations, 1016 Duke St., Alexandria, VA 22314.

SALES, MARKETING, AND MERCHANDISING

• •

Buyer and Merchandise Manager

Job Description

"I came, I saw, I shopped." This modern version of Julius Caesar's immortal proclamation seems to be the password of today's American consumer. Wholesale and retail buyers are no exception. Buyers are usually supervised by merchandise managers, who set general pricing policies for their department or store. Whether they are buying appliances, clothing, or machinery, they seek the best available merchandise at the lowest possible price. Working with sales and marketing managers, they also determine how the merchandise will be distributed and marketed.

Buyers working for large and mid-size firms usually specialize in acquiring one or two lines of merchandise. However, buyers working for small stores may purchase their complete stock of merchandise. Buyers in wholesale firms purchase goods directly from manufacturers or from other wholesalers. Retail buyers purchase goods from wholesalers or directly from manufacturers, for resale to the public.

Buyers determine which products will sell, and it is essential that they be knowledgeable about the products they are buying and that they know what will appeal to consumers. These skills are usually developed through several years of experience as an assistant buyer, which is an entry-level position. In order to purchase the best selection, buyers must be familiar with the merchandise, its manufacturers and distributors, and its sales record. To learn about merchandise, they read industry periodicals, attend trade shows and conferences, and visit manufacturers' showrooms.

Traditionally, buyers have relied on inventory counts to determine which products were selling. Today, computerized systems have simplified many of the routine buying functions, a major step in improving the efficiency and profitability of wholesale and retail firms. Cash registers connected to computer terminals allow firms to maintain centralized, up-to-date sales and inventory records. Prices, colors, and model numbers are recorded through the use of bar codes or magnetic strips attached to the goods. This information can then be used to produce daily or weekly sales reports.

The process of ordering goods varies by firm. Orders may be placed during buying trips or when wholesalers and manufacturers' representatives visit the buyers' home offices to display their merchandise.

Many buyers and merchandise managers assist in the planning and implementation of advertising and sales promotion strategies. Working with advertising personnel to create the ad campaign, they choose the media in which the advertisement will be placed: newspapers, radio, television, direct mail, or a combination of these. Retail buyers often visit the selling floor to see that the goods are being displayed properly.

Buyers and merchandise managers frequently work odd hours because of special sales and conferences. They may have to work evenings and weekends to complete work on time. This is especially true prior to holiday seasons. Substantial travel is often required, and most buyers often spend at least several days a month on the road.

Qualifications

Job applicants usually begin as assistant buyers or trainees. Educational requirements for entry-level positions vary with the size of the organization. Large stores and distributors seek applicants who have completed high school and who have completed an associate program at a junior college. However, many firms promote their sales employees to assistant buyer positions.

Those who find that they are being rejected for the buyer training programs because they do not have enough education can seek a position in sales and, once employed, apply to management for entrance into a training program.

Income and Advancement

Annual salaries of buyers range from approximately $26,000 to $34,000, with buyers employed by very large organizations earning more than $56,585. Experienced buyers may advance by moving to a department that manages a larger volume or by becoming a merchandise manager. Buyers and merchandise managers receive a variety of perks in addition to standard corporate benefits, including cash bonuses based on their performance and discounts on merchandise bought from the employer. They also have the opportunity to work their way up into top management positions with their firms.

Where to Get More Information

General information about a career in retailing is available from:

National Retail Federation, 100 W. 31st St., New York, NY 10001.

Insurance Agent and Broker

Job Description

Insurance agents and brokers help individuals or companies select the right insurance policies for their needs. They sell policies that provide financial protection against loss. They plan for the financial security of individuals, families, and businesses, and advise about insurance protection for automobiles, homes, businesses, or other properties. They prepare reports, maintain records, and help policy-holders settle insurance claims.

Insurance agents may work for one company or as independent agents selling for several companies. Insurance brokers do not sell for a particular company but place insurance policies for their clients with the company that offers the best rate and coverage.

Insurance comes in many forms: life, property/casualty, disability, and long-term care. Life insurance agents offer policies that pay survivors when a policyholder dies. Property/casualty insurance agents and brokers sell policies that protect individuals and businesses from financial loss as a result of automobile accidents, fire or theft, or other losses. Property/casualty insurance can also cover workers' compensation, product liability, or medical malpractice. Many agents also sell health insurance policies covering the costs of hospital and medical care or loss of income due to illness or injury.

An increasing number of insurance agents and brokers offer comprehensive financial planning services to their clients, such as retirement planning counseling. Many agents and brokers are licensed to sell mutual funds, annuities, and other securities. Most insurance agents and brokers spent a great deal of time outside their offices, traveling locally to meet with clients and prospects. They generally arrange their own hours of work, and often schedule evening and weekend appointments for the convenience of clients.

Qualifications

Employers prefer to hire high school graduates with potential or proven sales ability or those who have been successful in other types of work. In fact, most entrants have transferred from other occupations.

Community or junior college courses in business, finance, mathematics, and accounting provide a good background for a position as an insurance agent or broker.

Insurance agents and brokers should be enthusiastic, outgoing, self-confident, disciplined, hardworking, and able to communicate effectively. They should be able to inspire customer confidence and have the initiative to locate new clients.

Income and Advancement

Salaried insurance sales workers earned median salaries of $30,100 in 1992. The middle 50 percent earned between $20,900 and $42,200 a year, while the top 10 percent earned $64,600 a year and more. Most independent agents are paid on a commission only, whereas sales workers who are employees of an agency may be paid by salary only, salary plus commission, or salary plus bonus.

An insurance agent who shows sales ability and leadership may become a sales manager in a local office. A few advance to agency superintendent or executive positions. Some establish their own independent agencies or brokerage firms.

Where to Get More Information

National Association of Life Underwriters, 1922 F St., NW, Washington, DC 20006.

Independent Insurance Agents of America, 127 S. Peyton St., Alexandria, VA 22314.

National Association of Professional Insurance Agents, 400 N. Washington Ave., Alexandria, VA 22314.

Manufacturers' and Wholesale Sales Representative

Job Description

Name any product—from appliances to zippers—and you will probably find a manufacturers' and wholesale sales representative selling it.

Sales representatives market their company's products to manufacturers, wholesale and retail businesses, government agencies, and institutions of all kinds. The primary job of these workers is to interest wholesale and retail buyers and purchasing agents in their merchandise.

Sales representatives have different titles. Those representing manufacturers are known as manufacturers' representatives. Those selling technical products are usually called industrial sales engineers. Sales workers who are self-employed are known as manufacturers' agents.

Manufacturers' and wholesale sales representatives spend a large part of their time visiting prospective buyers. They show samples or catalogs that describe items that their company stocks, and they inform customers about prices, availability, and ways in which their products can save money and improve productivity.

Sales engineers sell products whose installation and use require a great deal of technical expertise and support, such as machinery, computers, copiers, and telecommunications systems. They may recommend improved materials for a company's manufacturing process, draw up plans of proposed machinery layout, and explain cost savings from the use of their equipment. Sales representatives who do have the technical background may attend sales presentations to explain and answer technical questions. After the sale, sales representatives may make follow-up visits to ensure that the equipment is functioning properly and, where necessary, help train customers' employees to operate and maintain new equipment.

Some manufacturers' and wholesale sales representatives travel extensively, often remaining away from home for days or weeks at a time. Others work near their home base and do most of their traveling by automobile. Most sales representatives have the freedom to set their own schedule of arranging appointments.

Two out of every three sales representatives work in wholesale trade, mostly for distributors of machinery and equipment, food products, and motor vehicles and parts; others are employed in manufacturing and mining. In addition to those employed by a company, many are self-employed manufacturers' agents who work for a straight commission based on the value of their sales.

Qualifications

Many employers prefer to hire individuals with previous sales experience and consider sales ability and familiarity with brands more important than a degree. However, firms selling complex industrial products or systems often require a degree in science or engineering.

Many companies have formal training programs for beginners that last up to two years. In others, trainees take formal classroom instruction at the plant, followed by on-the-job training under the supervision of a field sales manager.

Manufacturers' and wholesale sales representatives should be persuasive, have a pleasant personality, have the ability to get along well with people, and be able to work independently.

Income and Advancement

Most employers use a combination of salary and commission or salary plus bonus. Median annual earnings of full-time manufacturers' and wholesale sales representatives are about $32,000, ranging from $22,300 to $46,500, with the top 10 percent earning more than $62,000.

Promotion may take the form of an assignment to larger accounts or an expanded territory where commissions are likely to be greater. Experienced sales representatives may move into positions as sales trainers for new employees. Those with outstanding sales records and leadership ability may advance to sales supervisor or district manager positions. Many go into business for themselves as manufacturers' agents.

Where to Get More Information

Sales and Marketing Management, Intl., Statler Office Tower, Cleveland, OH 44115.

Real Estate Agent, Broker, and Appraiser

Job Description

Anyone who has purchased or sold a home or an investment property probably has sought the help of a real estate agent, broker, and appraiser.

Real estate agents and brokers know the local housing market. They know which areas will fit their clients' needs and budgets. They are familiar with zoning regulations, tax laws, and financing sources; and they are knowledgeable negotiators between buyers and sellers. Brokers are independent business people who not only sell real estate owned by others but also rent and manage properties.

They also conduct title searches and often provide information on loans and financing procedures. Brokers also advertise properties and are involved with other business matters, such as insurance and the practice of law.

Real estate agents generally are independent salespeople who provide their services to a licensed broker on a contract basis. Most derive their income solely from commissions.

In selling real estate, brokers and agents generally first meet with potential buyers to get a feeling for the type of home they would like and can afford. Then they take the buyer to see a number of homes that are likely to meet his or her needs and income. Because buying real estate is one of the most important financial events in people's lives, and one of the most complex as well, agents have to meet several times with a prospective buyer to discuss properties.

Agents and brokers do more than just make sales. They spend a significant amount of time obtaining "listings" or owners' agreements to place properties for sale, and they spend a great deal of time on the phone gathering leads from various sources.

Most real estate agents and brokers sell residential properties. Some, usually in large firms, sell commercial, industrial, or other types of real estate. Real estate transactions call for complex financial arrangements, so parties to the transactions usually seek the advice of real estate appraisers. An appraisal, an estimate of the quality and value of the property, may be used by sellers to set a competitive price, by lending institutions to determine the market value of the property for the purpose of a mortgage loan, or by local governments to determine the assessed value for tax purposes. Many appraisers are employed by banks, savings and loan associations, and mortgage companies, while others work for real estate appraisal firms.

Most real estate agents, brokers, and appraisers are self-employed and work on a commission basis. Most real estate firms are relatively small. Large firms may have several hundred real estate agents operating out of many branch offices. Franchised real estate agencies have become more prevalent in recent years, operating much like fast food operations where the broker pays a fee in exchange for the privilege of using the wider facilities of a well-known parent organizations.

Qualifications

Every state and the District of Columbia require that agents and brokers be licensed. Prospective agents must be high school graduates, be at least 18 years of age, and pass a written examination. In addition, most states require candidates for the license to complete at least 30 hours of classroom instruction. For a broker's license, at least 90 hours of classroom instruction are required.

Many homemakers and retired persons are attracted to real estate sales by the flexible and part-time work schedules available. Many transfer into real estate sales from a variety of occupations.

Many firms offer formal training programs for both beginners and experienced agents. The National Association of Realtors, through local member real estate boards, sponsors courses covering the fundamentals of the field.

Income and Advancement

The main source of income for real estate agents and brokers is derived from commissions; few receive salary. Commissions vary according to the type of property and its value.

Real estate agents, brokers, and appraisers who usually work full time have median weekly earnings of $515. The middle 50 percent earn between $335 and $825, while the top 10 percent earn more than $1,247 a week. The most successful agents and brokers earn considerably more. Income usually increases as an agent gains experience, but individual ability, economic conditions, and the type and location of the property also affect earnings.

Experienced agents can advance in large firms to sales or general manager positions. Those who have received their broker's license may open their own offices. Others with experience and training in estimating property values may become real estate appraisers.

Where to Get More Information

National Association of Realtors, 777 14th St., NW, Washington, DC 20005.

Appraisal Institute, 875 N. Michigan Ave., Chicago, IL 60611.

American Society of Appraisers, P.O. Box 17265, Washington, DC 20041.

Securities and Financial Services Sales Representative

Job Description

When investors—whether they are individuals or large institutions—buy or sell stocks, bonds, shares in mutual funds, annuities, certificates of deposit, or other financial products, they usually use securities sales representatives to handle the transactions. These representatives are often called registered representatives, account executives, or brokers.

Securities sales representatives must meet state licensing requirements, which generally include passing the examination and, in some cases, furnishing a personal bond. They must also register as representatives of their firm according to regulations for the securities exchanges where they do business or the National Association of Securities Dealers (NASD). Beginners must also pass the General Securities Registered Representative Examination, administered by the NASD. Most employers provide on-the-job training to help securities sales representatives meet the requirements for registration.

Financial services sales representatives, like securities sales representatives, work with all kinds of financial services and products. Their customers, however, are generally businesses rather than individuals. They call on various businesses to solicit applications for loans and new deposit accounts for banks or savings and loan associations. They also locate and contact prospective customers to present their firm's financial services and to ascertain the customer's banking needs.

Qualifications

Although a college education for beginning applicants is increasingly important, especially in the larger securities firms, many employers prefer to hire individuals with sales experience, particularly those who have the maturity and ability to work independently. Especially desirable are those who have had experience working on commission in such areas as real estate or insurance. Most entrants to this occupation transfer from other jobs. Employers seek applicants who have good communications skills, are well-groomed, and have a strong desire to succeed. Self-confidence and an ability to handle frequent rejections also are important ingredients for success. High school business or economic courses are desirable, as are attendance at junior and community colleges or private business schools.

Income and Advancement

Experienced securities and financial services sales representatives averaged about $128,553 in 1993.

Trainees usually are paid a salary until they meet licensing and registration requirements. After registration, a few firms continue to pay a salary until the new representative's commissions increase to a stated amount. The salaries paid during training usually range from $1,200 to $1,500 a month. After candidates are licensed and registered, their earnings depend on commissions from the sale or purchase of stocks and bonds, life insurance, or other securities for customers. Most firms provide sales representative with a steady income by paying a "draw against commissions"—that is, a minimum salary based on the commissions that they can be expected to earn.

Some experienced sales representatives become branch office managers and supervise other sales representatives. A few advance to top management positions or become partners in their firms.

Where to Get More Information

Career information may be obtained from the personnel departments of individual securities firms, banks and other financial institutions. Information also can be obtained by contacting:

Securities Industry Association, 120 Broadway, New York, NY 10006.

TECHNOLOGY

●●

Air Traffic Controller

Job Description

Seated comfortably in a modern airplane, reading a magazine, watching a movie, or just relaxing, few people give any thought to the complex system on the ground that is guiding their flight over land or water. Regardless of the length of the trip, safety is in the hands of air traffic controllers from the minute passengers enter the plane until they disembark at their destination. The controllers are the guardians of the airways. They use their training, skills, and dedication to shepherd planes through the nation's airways 24 hours a day. Their immediate concern is safety, but controllers also must direct planes efficiently to minimize delays. Some regulate airport traffic; others regulate flights between airports. Relying on radar as well as visual observation, they closely monitor each plane to maintain a safe distance between aircraft while in the air. They also guide crews operating planes between the hangars and runways.

During arrival or departure, each plane is handled by several controllers. As a plane approaches the airport, the pilot radios ahead to inform the terminal of the aircraft's presence. If the way is clear, the controller directs the pilot to a runway. If the airport is busy, the plane is fitted into a traffic pattern with other aircraft waiting to land. Once the plane has landed, a ground controller in the tower directs it along the taxiways to its assigned gate.

A similar procedure is used for departures. The ground controller directs the plane to the proper runway. The local controller then informs the pilot about the weather, visibility, and the speed and direction of the wind, and issues runway clearance for takeoff. Once in the air, the plane is guided out of the airport by the departure controller. After each plane takes off, airport tower controllers notify enroute controllers, who take over next. There are 24 enroute control centers around the country, each employing 300 to 700 controllers. Airplanes generally fly along designed routes; each center is assigned a certain airspace containing many different routes. Enroute controllers working in teams are responsible for a section of the center's airspace. For example, a team might be responsible for all planes flying between 30 and 100 miles south of an airport and at an altitude between 7,000 and 20,000 feet.

As a plane approaches a team's airspace, the new team takes over from the previous controlling team. Radar controllers warn pilots about nearby planes, weather conditions, and other hazards. As the flight progresses, the team responsible for the aircraft notifies the next team in charge. The plane is handed from one sector to another until it arrives safely at its destination.

In addition to airport towers and enroute centers, air traffic controllers also work in flight service stations operated at more than 100 locations. They provide pilots with information on the station's particular area, including terrain, preflight and inflight weather information, suggested routes, and other information important to the safety of the flight. Flight station controllers assist pilots in emergency situations and participate in searches for missing or overdue aircraft.

Qualifications

Air traffic controller trainees, selected through the federal civil service system, must pass a written test that measures their ability to learn controller's duties. Abstract reasoning and three-dimensional visual aptitudes are measured. A college degree is not necessary, but applicants must have three years of general work experience and must not have reached their 31st birthday. Those 31 years old and over are eligible for positions at flight service stations. Candidates must be articulate because directions to pilots must be given quickly and clearly.

Successful applicants receive a combination of on-the-job and formal training to learn the fundamentals of the airway system, FAA regulations, controller equipment, and aircraft performance characteristics. They receive 11 to 13 weeks of intensive screening and training at the FAA academy in Oklahoma City.

New controllers, assigned at airports, begin by supplying pilots with basic flight data and airport information. They then advance to ground controller, then local controller, departure controller, and, finally, arrival controller. Controllers can transfer to jobs in different locations or advance to supervisory positions, including management or staff jobs in air traffic control and top administrative jobs in the FAA.

Income and Advancement

Starting air traffic controllers earn about $22,000 a year. A controller's salary is determined by both the worker's job and the complexity of the particular facility. Earnings are higher at facilities where traffic patterns are more complex. In 1992, controllers averaged about $53,800 a year. Supervisors earn more, depending on the responsibilities and size of the facility. Controllers have the opportunity to move into staff jobs in air traffic control and top administrative jobs in the FAA.

Where to Get More Information

General information and literature about controllers and instructions for submitting an application are available from any U.S. Office of Personnel Management Job Information Center. Look under U.S. Government of Personnel Management in your local telephone directory.

Broadcast Technician

Job Description

All the radio and television producers, directors, writers, and actors in the world could not put on a single program without the broadcast technicians working behind the scenes.

Working on the other side of the microphones and cameras, broadcast technicians install, test, repair, and operate the electronic equipment used to record and transmit radio and television programs. They work with television cameras, microphones, tape recorders, light and sound effects, transmitters, antennas, and other equipment.

In the control room of a radio or television broadcasting studio, these technicians operate equipment that regulates the signal strength, clarity, and range of color and sounds of the material being recorded or broadcast. They operate the control panels and, with the use of telephone headsets, give technical direction to personnel in the studio.

Broadcast technicians in small stations perform a variety of duties. In large stations and at the networks, they are more specialized. Transmitter operators monitor and log outgoing signals and operate transmitters. Maintenance technicians set up, adjust, service, and repair electronic equipment. Audio control engineers regulate sound pickup and transmission, and video control engineers regulate the quality of the television pictures. Recording engineers operate and maintain video and sound recording equipment. Television news coverage requires so much electronic equipment, and the technology is changing so fast, that many stations assign technicians exclusively to news.

Technicians in large stations and the networks usually work a 40-hour week but may occasionally work overtime, under great pressure, to meet broadcast deadlines. Technicians in small stations routinely work more than 40 hours a week. Evening, weekend, and holiday work is usual because most stations are on the air 18 to 24 hours a day, seven days a week.

Qualifications

The best way to prepare for a broadcast technician job, particularly for those who hope to advance to supervisory positions or to jobs in large stations and at the networks, is to complete technical school or community college training in broadcast technology or electronics.

Anyone who operates and maintains broadcast transmitters in radio and television stations must have a restricted radiotelephone operator's permit, according to federal law. Beginners learn skills on the job from experienced technicians. Many employers pay tuition and expenses for courses or seminars to help technicians keep abreast of developments in the field.

Broadcast technicians need the electronic training and hand coordination necessary to operate technical equipment, and they generally complete specialized programs. They must possess an aptitude for working with electrical and mechanical systems and equipment, and have the manual dexterity and the ability to perform tasks requiring precise, coordinated hand movements.

Income and Advancement

Television stations usually pay higher salaries than radio stations; commercial broadcasting usually pays more than educational broadcasting; and stations in large markets pay more than those in small ones. Salaries range from $18,000 a year in the smallest markets to $45,000 a year in the largest markets. Experienced technicians may become supervisors or chief engineers. Salaries in stations and studio that are unionized are governed by negotiated contracts and provide higher wages and better benefits than non-union companies.

Where to Get More Information

For information about licensing, write to:

Federal Communications Commission, 1919 M St., NW, Washington, DC 20554.

For information about careers for broadcast technicians, write to:

National Association of Broadcasters Employment Clearing-house, 1771 N St., NW, Washington, DC 20036.

For a list of schools that offer programs or courses in broadcasting, contact:

Broadcast Education Association, National Association of Broadcasters, 1771 N St., NW, Washington, DC 20036.

For information on certification, contact:

Society of Broadcast Engineers, 8445 Keystone at the Crossing, Indianapolis, IN 46240.

Computer Programmer

Job Description

A computer is no better than its programs. Computer programmers write, update, and maintain the detailed instructions (called programs or software) that list in a logical order the steps that computers must execute.

In many large organizations, programmers follow descriptions prepared by systems analysts who have carefully studied the task that the computer system is going to perform. These descriptions list the input required, the steps the computer must follow to process data, and the desired objective. Programmers in software development companies work directly with experts from various fields to create new software packages for specific applications, such as graphics, computer-aided design (CAD), animation, and educational instruction.

Regardless of setting, programmers write specific programs by breaking down each step into a logical series of instructions the computer can follow. They then code these instructions in a programming language for business applications, scientific programming, or one of the more advanced artificial intelligence languages.

Some programmers may write completely new programs, but most programming work involves the updating and modification of existing programs. Finally, programmers prepare instructions for the computer operators who will run the programs.

Programs vary with the type of information to be accessed. For example, the data involved in updating school records is different from that required to simulate a flight on a pilot trainee's monitor. Programmers often are grouped into two broad types: applications programmers and systems programmers. Applications programmers usually are oriented toward business, engineering, or science, writing software to handle specific jobs—for example, programs used in inventory control systems, to guide a missile after it has been fired, or in word processing to be used in a business setting. Systems programmers maintain the software that controls the operations of entire computer systems.

Qualifications

There are no universal training requirements for programmers because computer applications are so widespread and varied that employers' needs also vary greatly. Computer programming is taught at public and vocational schools, community and junior colleges, and universities. High schools in many parts of the country also offer introductory courses in data processing.

Employers using computers for scientific or engineering applications prefer college graduates who have degrees in computer science, mathematics, engineering, or the physical sciences. However, a large number of employers who use computers for such activities as inventory control, correspondence, records, personnel, finance, and other nontechnical applications generally do not require a four-year college degree. Many firms, however, prefer people who have had courses in programming and business. Also helpful are experience in accounting and management, and other business skills. Employers look for people who can think logically and who are capable of performing exacting analytical work.

Beginning programmers may spend their first weeks on the job attending training classes. After initial instruction, they may work alone on simple assignments or on a team with more experienced programmers.

Income and Advancement

Median earnings of programmers who worked full time in 1992 were about $35,600 a year, with the highest 10 percent earning more than $58,000. On average, systems programmers earn more than application programmers. Programmers employed by very large firms can earn more.

Although many employers prefer to hire applicants with experience in the field, some promote workers, such as computer operators, who have taken courses in programming. For skilled workers, the prospects for advancement are good. In large organizations, they may be promoted to lead programmer and be given supervisory responsibilities that can ultimately lead to a managerial position.

Where to Get More Information

Institute for the Certification of Computer Professionals, 2200 E. Devon Ave., Des Plaines, IL 60018.

Drafter

Job Description

Drafters prepare technical drawings used by production workers to build office buildings, houses, bridges, and other structures. They also prepare drawings for aircraft, industrial machinery, and other manufactured products. Their drawings portray technical details of the products and structures with exact dimensions from all sides showing the specific materials to be used, procedures to be followed, and other information needed to complete the project.

Drafters prepare and fill in technical details, using drawings, rough sketches, specifications, and calculations made by engineers, surveyors, architects, and scientists.

There are two methods by which drawings are prepared. In the traditional method, drafters sit at drawing boards and, using compasses, dividers, protractors, triangles, and other drafting devices, prepare the drawing manually. Today, drafters also use computer-aided drafting systems (CAD), working with computers to create the drawings on a video screen. The drawing can then be printed or just stored electronically. As the cost of CAD systems drops, it is likely that in the not-too-distant future, almost all drafters will use CAD systems.

Many drafters specialize. For example, aeronautical drafters prepare engineering drawings used for the manufacture of aircraft and missiles. Electrical drafters draw wiring and layout diagrams used by workers who erect, install, and repair electrical equipment and wiring in power plants, electrical distribution systems, and buildings. Electronic drafters draw wiring diagrams, circuit board diagrams, schematics, and layout drawings used in the manufacture and installation of electronic equipment. Civil drafters prepare drawings and topographical and relief maps used in civil engineering projects, such as highways, bridges, flood control projects, and water and sewage systems. Mechanical drafters draw details and diagrams of machinery and mechanical devices.

Qualifications

Employers prefer applicants for drafting positions who have post–high school training in technical institutes or junior and community colleges, and who have well-developed drafting and mechanical drawing skills, a solid background in computer-aided design techniques, and courses in mathematics, science, or engineering technology.

Those planning careers in drafting should be able to draw freehand three-dimensional objects and do detailed work accurately and neatly. Artistic ability is helpful in some specialized fields. In addition, prospective drafters should be able to work closely with engineers, surveyors, architects, and other workers.

Income and Advancement

Median annual earnings of drafters who work year-round and full time are about $27,400. The middle 50 percent earn between

$20,600 and $33,500 annually and about 10 percent earn more than $43,500.

Where to Get More Information

Your local state employment service office can provide information about jobs opportunities for drafters.

Engineering Technician

Job Description

Engineering technicians assist engineers and scientists involved in research and development, manufacturing, sales, construction, and customer service. Those who work in research and development build or set up equipment, prepare and conduct experiments, calculate or record the results, and assist engineers in other ways. They also assist in routine design work, often using computer-aided design equipment.

Technicians who work in manufacturing follow the general directions of engineers. They may prepare specifications for materials, devise and run tests to ensure product quality, or study ways to improve manufacturing efficiency.

Engineering technicians also work as field representatives of manufacturers, wholesalers, or retailers. They help customers install, test, operate, and maintain complex technical equipment, and may write repair or operating manuals.

Civil engineering technicians help civil engineers plan and build highways, buildings, bridges, dams, wastewater treatment systems, and other structures, and do related surveys and studies. Some inspect water and wastewater treatment plants to ensure that pollution control requirements are met. Others estimate construction costs and specify materials to be used.

Electronics engineering technicians help develop, manufacture, and service electronic equipment, such as radios, radar, sonar, television, industrial and medical control devices, navigational equipment, and computers.

Industrial engineering technicians study the efficient use of personnel, materials, and machines in factories, stores, repair shops, and offices. They prepare layouts of machinery and equipment, plan the flow of work, make statistical studies, and analyze production costs.

Mechanical engineering technicians help engineers design and develop machinery and other equipment by making sketches and rough layouts. They prepare drawings of the assembly process and estimate labor costs, equipment, and plant space. Some test and inspect machines and equipment in manufacturing departments or work with engineers to eliminate production problems.

Qualifications

Although no formal training is necessary for some engineering technician jobs, most employers prefer to hire someone who will require less on-the-job training or supervision. Training is available at technical institutes, junior and community colleges, extension divisions of colleges and universities, and public and private vocational schools. In some cases, training can be obtained on the job or through apprenticeship programs or correspondence schools.

Prospective engineering technicians should take as many high school science and math courses as possible. They should be able to work well with others since they are often part of a team of engineers and other technicians. Those in sales and service should be able to work independently and deal effectively with customers.

Income and Advancement

Engineering technicians in private industry earn from $28,800 to $41,400, depending on the size of the organization and the level of the position. Engineering technicians can eventually become supervisors, and some go on to become engineers.

Where to Get More Information

JETS-Guidance, 1420 King St., Alexandria, VA 22314.

Science Technician

Job Description

Applying the use of the principles and theories of science to solve problems, science technicians use their knowledge and skills to solve problems in research and development. Unlike scientists, technicians are concerned with the more practical aspects of research as they investigate, invent, and help improve products. In their work, they make extensive use of computers, robotics, and high technology.

Technicians use many complex laboratory instruments to monitor experiments, calculate and record results, and develop conclusions. Science technicians are employed in a variety of fields.

Agricultural technicians work with agricultural scientists in food and fiber research, production, and processing. Some do animal breeding and nutrition work.

Biological technicians work with biologists, studying living organisms. Many help conduct medical research, helping to find cures for specific diseases, or they may help conduct pharmaceutical research.

Chemical technicians work with chemists and chemical engineers, developing and using chemicals and related products and equipment. Most are involved in research and development, testing, and other laboratory work.

Nuclear technicians operate nuclear test and research equipment, monitor radiation, and assist physicists and nuclear engineers in research.

Petroleum technicians measure and record physical and geologic conditions in oil or gas wells through the use of instruments that are lowered into wells, and by analysis of the soil content of wells to determine oil and mineral content.

Other science technicians assist meteorologists, oceanographers, or space scientists.

Qualifications

Most employers prefer applicants who have at least two years of specialized training. Many community colleges, junior colleges, and technical institutes offer associate degree programs in a specific technology or a more general education in science and mathematics. Some schools offer cooperative education programs, enabling students to work at a local firm and attend classes in alternate terms. Some companies offer formal on-the-job training. Those interested in careers as science technicians should take high school courses in science and math. Because computers are commonly used in research and development, computer skills are valuable.

Income and Advancement

Annual earnings of science technicians range between $18,900 and $33,400 or more. About 10 percent earn more than $42,400. Salary schedules vary according to the nature of the employer and the qualifications of the applicant. Universities, pharmaceutical firms, mineral exploration organizations, and others may vary in their requirements.

Where to Get More Information

American Chemical Society, Education Division, 1155 16th St., NW, Washington, DC 20036.

TRANSPORTATION AND MATERIAL MOVING

• •

Aircraft Pilot

Job Description

Pilots fly a wide variety of aircraft to carry out many different tasks. Most pilots transport passengers, cargo, and mail; others dust crops, spread seed for reforestation, take photographs, and test airplanes. Helicopter pilots are involved in police work, offshore exploration, firefighting, evacuation and rescue efforts, logging operations, construction work, and weather station operations. Some also transport passengers.

On multiengine aircraft, two pilots usually make up the cockpit crew, with the most experienced pilot, the captain, in command and supervising other crew members. The copilot assists in communicating with air traffic controllers, monitoring the instruments, and flying the aircraft. Most large aircraft have a third pilot, the flight engineer, who assists the other pilots by monitoring and operating many of the instruments and systems.

Before departure, pilots confer with flight dispatchers and weather forecasters and, based on information received from them, choose a route, altitude, and speed. Pilots guide the plane along the planned route and are monitored by the air traffic control stations they pass along the way. They continuously scan the instrument panel to check their fuel supply, the condition of the engines, cabin pressure, hydraulics, and other systems. They may request a change in altitude to find a stronger tailwind or a weaker headwind to save fuel and increase speed. Special navigation radios give pilots precise information that, with the help of special maps, tells them their exact position. Other instruments provide direction to a point just above the end of a runway, enabling pilots to land completely "blind."

Pilots employed by businesses that use their own aircraft may have other duties, such as loading the plane, handling passenger luggage to ensure a balanced load, and supervising refueling. Some pilots are instructors, teaching students how to fly in dual-control planes. A few specially trained pilots employed by airlines are "examiners" or "check pilots" who make sure that pilots are proficient.

Qualifications

All pilots who transport passengers or cargo must have a commercial pilot's license with an instrument rating issued by the FAA. Helicopter pilots must hold a commercial pilot's certificate with a helicopter rating. To qualify, applicants must be at least 18 years old and have at least 250 hours of flight experience. They also must pass a strict physical examination and have 20-20 vision with or without glasses, good hearing, and no physical handicaps that could impair their performance. They also must pass a written test.

Flying can be learned in military or civilian flying schools. There are about 600 civilian flying schools, including some colleges that offer courses. Pilots hired by the airlines must be high school graduates. Most airlines, however, require a minimum of two years of college.

Income and Advancement

Advancement usually depends on seniority provisions of union contracts. After two to seven years, flight engineers advance to copilot; after five to 15 years, to captain.

Average salaries for airline pilots are about $80,000 a year; for copilots, $65,000; and for captains, $107,000. Some senior captains on the largest aircraft earn as much as $165,000. Earnings depend on such factors as the type, size, and maximum speed of the plane, and the number of hours and miles flown.

Generally, pilots working outside the airlines earn lower salaries. Average salaries for chief pilots are about $62,000 a year. Pilots who fly business aircraft earn approximately $57,900; co-pilots, about $42,000 a year.

Where to Get More Information

Information about jobs with a particular airline may be obtained by writing to the personnel manager of the airline.

For addresses of airline companies, contact:

Future Aviation Professionals of America, 4291 J. Memorial Dr., Atlanta, GA 30032. Or call 1-800-JET-JOBS.

For information on airline pilots, contact:

Airline Pilots Association of America, 1625 Massachusetts Ave., Washington, DC 20036.

Air Transport Association of America, 1709 York Ave., NW, Washington, DC 20006.

For information on helicopter pilots, contact:

Helicopter Association, Intl., 1619 Duke St., Alexandria, VA 22314.

For a copy of *List of Certificated Pilot Schools*, write to:

Superintendent of Documents, U.S. Government Printing Office, Washington, DC 20402.

Bus Driver

Job Description

Bus drivers provide transportation for millions of Americans every day. Intercity drivers transport people between towns, cities, and states. Local transit bus drivers move passengers to and from schools and institutions.

Drivers answer questions about schedules, routes, and transfer points; collect fares; check passes; and makes necessary announcements to the passengers. They must be alert to prevent accidents and to avoid sudden stops or swerves that jar passengers. School bus drivers must exercise particular caution, and they must know and reinforce rules of the school system.

Local transit drivers submit daily trip reports with a record of tickets and fares received, trips made, and significant delays in schedules; and they report any mechanical problems they experience. Intercity drivers who drive across state or national boundaries must comply with U.S. Department of Transportation requirements. These include completing vehicle inspection reports and recording distances traveled and the periods of time they spend driving, performing duties, and off duty.

Regular local transit drivers usually have a five-day workweek, including Saturdays and Sundays. Some work evenings and after midnight to accommodate commuters. Many work "split shifts," with time off in between.

Qualifications

Qualifications and standards are established by state and federal regulations, which require that all drivers who operate vehicles designed to transport 16 or more passengers obtain a commercial driver's license from the state in which they live.

To be licensed, applicants for a commercial driver's license must pass a knowledge test and demonstrate that they have all the skills necessary to operate a commercial motor vehicle safely. They are also required to pass a behind-the-wheel road test in the type of vehicle that they will be operating.

Interstate drivers must meet additional qualifications. They must be at least 21 years old and pass a physical examination. Many interstate and public transit bus companies prefer applicants who are at least 24 years of age, and some require several years of bus or truck driving experience.

Income and Advancement

In 1993, according to the American Public Transit Association, local transit bus drivers in metropolitan areas with more than two million inhabitants were paid a median top hourly wage of $16.41 by companies with more than 1,000 employees, and $14.08 by those with fewer than 1,000 employees. In smaller areas, they had a median top hourly wage of $12.13 in areas with between 250,000 and 500,000 residents.

Earnings of intercity bus drivers depend primarily on the number of miles they drive. According to limited information, in 1992, beginning intercity drivers worked about six months out of the year and earned about $22,000, while many senior drivers who worked year-round earned more than $48,000.

According to a survey by the Educational Research Service, the average rate for school bus drivers employed by public school systems is about $11 an hour during the school year.

Most intercity and many local transit drivers are members of the Amalgamated Transit Union. Local transit bus drivers in New York and several other large cities belong to the Transport Workers Union of America. Some belong to the United Transportation Union and the International Brotherhood of Teamsters.

Where to Get More Information

For further information on employment opportunities, contact local transit systems, intercity buslines, school systems, or the local office of the state employment service. Further information is available from the following:

National School Transportation Association, P.O. Box 2639, Springfield, VA 22152.

American Public Transit Association, 1201 New York Ave., NW, Suite 400, Washington, DC 20001.

Material-Moving-Equipment Operator

Job Description

Workers who move equipment, construction materials, earth, logs, petroleum products, grain, coal, and other manufactured goods are known as material-moving-equipment operators. Those who operate bulldozers, cranes, loaders, and similar equipment are called construction equipment operators, even though they may work in the mining, logging, utilities, and other industries. Others operate industrial trucks and tractors and equipment used in manufacturing plants and warehouses.

Crane and tower operators lift and move materials, machinery, or other heavy objects, using mechanical or hydraulic booms and tower cable equipment.

Excavation and loading machine operators run and tend power scoops, shovels, or buckets to remove or level and grade earth. They also operate trench excavators and road graders.

Hoist and winch operators lift and pull loads by using power-operated equipment. Operating engineers are qualified to operate more than one type of construction equipment.

Other material-moving-equipment operators tend air compressors or pumps at construction sites. Some operate oil or natural gas pumps and compressors at oil and gas wells and on oil and gas pipelines; and others operate ship loading and unloading equipment, conveyors, hoists, and other kinds of specialized material-handling equipment, such as mine or railroad tank car unloading equipment.

Qualifications

Operation of material-moving equipment is usually learned on the job. Employers prefer to hire high school graduates, although, for some equipment, applicants with less education may be accepted.

Mechanical aptitude and high school training in automobile mechanics are helpful because workers may perform some maintenance on their machines.

Some construction equipment operators are trained in a three-year apprenticeship program administered by a union-management program. Private vocational schools offer instruction in the operation of certain types of construction equipment. Completion of such a program may help a person get a job as a trainee or apprentice. Those considering such training should check the reputation and credentials of the school among employers in the area.

Income and Advancement

Earnings for material-moving-equipment operators vary considerably. Median earnings of all operators are about $432 a week; the middle 50 percent earn between $317 and $590, and about 10 percent earn more than $765 a week. Median weekly earnings of crane and tower operators are about $570; of excavation and loading machine operators, $441.

Where to Get More Information

For further information about apprenticeships or work opportunities for construction equipment operators, contact a local of the International Union of Operating Engineers or the local office of your state employment service.

For general information, contact:

Associated Builders and Contractors, 729 15th St., NW, Washington, DC 20005.

International Union of Operating Engineers, 1125 17th St., NW, Washington, DC 20036.

Industrial Truck Association, 1750 K St., NW, Washington, DC 20006.

Rail Transportation Worker

Job Description

Rail transportation workers are responsible for the movement of passengers and freight by America's trains, subways, and streetcars. Their jobs vary depending upon the work they are called on to perform.

Railroads employ the highest-skilled workers, such as locomotive engineers and rail yard engineers. These workers operate locomotives in yards, stations, and over the track between distant stations and yards. Locomotive engineers operate trains carrying cargo and passengers between stations, while rail yard engineers move cars within yards to assemble or disassemble trains. Most engineers run diesel locomotives; a few run electric locomotives. Before and after each run, engineers check locomotives for mechanical problems. Minor adjustments are made on the spot, but major problems are reported to the engine shop supervisor.

Road conductors and yard conductors are in charge of the train and yard crews. Conductors assigned to freight trains keep records of each car's contents and destination and make sure that cars are added and removed at the proper points along the route. Conductors assigned to passenger trains collect tickets and fares and assist passengers.

Yard conductors supervise the crews that assemble and disassemble trains. Some cars are sent to special tracks for unloading, while others are moved to other tracks to await being made into trains destined for different destinations. Conductors tell engineers where to move cars, and they tell brake operators which cars to couple and uncouple and which switches to throw to divert the locomotive or cars to the proper track.

Brake operators play a crucial role in making locomotives and cars into trains. Working under the direction of conductors, they do the physical work involved in adding and removing cars at railroad stations and assembling and disassembling trains in railroad yards.

Subway operators control subway trains. When breakdowns or emergencies occur, operators contact their dispatcher or supervisor and may have to evacuate subway cars. To meet schedules, operators must control the amount of time spent at each station.

Street car operators drive electric-powered streetcars. They collect fares from passengers, and issue change and transfers. They also maintain schedules.

Qualifications

Most railroad workers begin as trainees for either engineer or brake operator jobs. Railroads prefer that applicants have a high school education and pass a physical examination, and that applicants for locomotive engineer jobs be at least 21 years old. Most beginning engineers undergo a six-month training program, which includes classroom and hands-on instruction in locomotive operation. At the end of the training period, trainee engineers must pass qualifying tests covering locomotive equipment, airbrake systems, fuel economy, train-handling techniques, and operating rules and regulations.

On most railroads, brake operators begin by making several trips with conductors and experienced operators to become familiar with the job.

Income and Advancement

Earnings of railroad transportation workers depend on the size of the train and type of service. According to the Brotherhood of Locomotive Engineers, in 1991, through-freight engineers averaged about $59,600 a year, passenger engineers about $57,900, way-freight engineers about $54,100, and yard engineers about $43,300 a year.

According to the Association of American Railroads, for the same period, annual earnings of conductors averaged $40,400 for through-freight and $35,200 for local and way-freight. Brake operators averaged about $33,600 for through-freight and $27,300 for local and way-freight. Yard brake operators averaged about $25,600.

Most rail transportation employees in yards work 40 hours a week and receive extra pay for overtime. On road service, most workers are paid according to miles traveled or hours worked, whichever leads to higher earnings. Most workers are members of unions, such as the Brotherhood of Locomotive Engineers, United

Transportation Union, Amalgamated Transit Union, or Transport Workers Union of North America.

Where to Get More Information

Information on employment opportunities for railroad transportation workers may be obtained from the employment offices of the various railroads and rail transit systems or from state employment security offices.

For general information about career opportunities in passenger transportation, contact:

American Public Transit Association, 1201 New York Ave., NW, Washington, DC 20005.

Truck Driver

Job Description

Nearly all goods are transported by truck during some of their journey from producers to consumers. They may be shipped between terminals or warehouses, or between cities by train, ship, or airplane. But truck drivers usually make the initial pickup from factories, consolidate cargo at terminals, and deliver merchandise from terminals to stores and homes.

Long-distance trips vary. On short "turnarounds," truck drivers deliver a load to a nearby city, pick up another loaded trailer, and drive it back to their home base the same day. Other runs take an entire day, requiring the driver to remain away from home overnight. On longer runs, drivers may haul loads from city to city for a week or more before returning home. Some companies use two drivers on very long runs. One drives while the other sleeps in a berth behind the cab. These "sleeper" runs may last for days, or even weeks, with the truck stopping only for fuel, food, loading, and unloading.

Long-distance drivers spend most of their working time behind the wheel, but may be required to unload their cargo. Drivers hauling special cargoes often load or unload their trucks, since they may be the only ones at the destination familiar with this procedure.

Some local truck drivers have sales and customer relations responsibilities. Called driver-sales workers or route drivers, they are responsible for delivering their employer's products, but they also represent the company. Their reaction to customer complaints and requests for special services can make the difference between a large order and loss of a customer. Route drivers also use their selling ability to increase sales and to gain additional customers.

The U.S. Department of Transportation governs work hours and other matters of trucking companies engaged in interstate commerce. For instance, a long-distance driver cannot be on duty for more than 60 hours in any seven-day period and cannot drive more than 10 hours following at least eight consecutive hours off duty.

Trucking companies employ nearly one-third of all drivers, and another one-third work for companies engaged in wholesale or retail trade. The rest are scattered throughout the economy, including government agencies. About 10 percent of truck drivers are self-employed. Of these, a significant number are owner-operators who either operate independently, serving a variety of businesses, or lease their services and trucks to a trucking company.

Qualifications

Qualifications and standards for truck drivers are set by state and federal regulations. All truck drivers must have a driver's license issued by the state in which they live. All drivers of trucks designed to carry at least 26,000 pounds, which includes most tractor-trailers as well as bigger straight trucks, are required to obtain a special commercial driver's license (CAL) from the state in which they live. A driver who is engaged in interstate commerce must be at least 21 years old and pass a physical examination. In addition, drivers must take a written examination on the Motor Carrier Safety Regulations of the U.S. Department of Transportation. Many trucking operations have higher standards, requiring that drivers be at least 25 years old and have driven trucks for three to five years. Many prefer to hire high school graduates and require annual physical examinations. High school driver-training courses are an asset, and courses in automotive mechanics may help drivers make minor roadside repairs. Many private and public technical-vocational schools offer tractor-trailer driver training programs.

Income and Advancement

Generally, local truck drivers are paid by the hour and receive extra pay for working overtime, usually after 40 hours. Long-distance drivers are usually paid primarily by the mile (the rate per mile can vary greatly from employer to employer), with their earnings increasing with mileage driven, seniority, and the size and type of truck. Most driver–sales workers receive a commission based on their sales in addition to an hourly wage.

Drivers employed by trucking companies have the highest earnings, averaging about $14.55 an hour in 1992. Most long-distance truck drivers operate tractor-trailers, and their earnings vary widely, from as little as $20,000 to over $40,000 annually.

Advancement of truck drivers is generally limited to driving runs that provide increased earnings or preferred schedules and working conditions. A local truck driver may advance to driving heavy or special types of trucks or transfer to long-distance driving. A few truck drivers may advance to dispatcher; to manager; or to traffic work, such as planning delivery schedules. Some long-distance truckers purchase a truck and go into business for themselves. Owner-operators should have good business sense.

Many truck drivers are members of the International Brotherhood of Teamsters. Some employed by companies outside the trucking industry are members of unions that represent the plant workers of the companies for which they work.

Where to Get More Information

Information on truck driver employment opportunities is available from local trucking companies and local offices of the state employment service.

Information on career opportunities may be obtained from:

American Trucking Associations, Inc., 2200 Mill Rd., Alexandria, VA 22314.